THE COMPLETE CRAYON BOOK

in color

CHESTER JAY ALKEMA
Associate Professor of Art
College of Arts and Sciences
Grand Valley State Colleges
Allendale, Michigan

STERLING PUBLISHING CO., Inc.,
New York

THE OAK TREE PRESS, Ltd., London and Sydney
SAUNDERS OF TORONTO, Ltd., Don Mills, Canada

BOOKS BY PROFESSOR ALKEMA

Alkema's Complete Guide to
    Creative Art for Young People
Aluminum and Copper Tooling
Complete Crayon Book
Crafting with Nature's Materials
Creative Paper Crafts in Color

Greeting Cards You Can Make
Masks
Monster Masks
Puppet-Making
Starting with Papier Mâché
Tissue Paper Creations

ACKNOWLEDGMENTS

The author offers special thanks to the young children of Wyoming Parkview School, Wyoming, Michigan, and to the many classroom teachers, teachers' aides and practice teachers associated with Grand Valley State College and Michigan State University; to the publishers of *Arts and Activities* for granting permission to use photographs and text material from published articles in the December, 1963 and November, 1964 issues; to the publishers of *Grade Teacher* for granting permission to use material from an article in the April, 1965 issue; to the publishers of *School Arts* for granting permission to use material from an article in the March, 1967 issue; and to the publishers of *The Instructor* for granting permission to use material from articles in the October, 1968 and November, 1968 issues.

He would like to thank the following for granting permission to photograph works of art which appear in this book: The American Crayon Company; and Dr. Richard Percy, Superintendent of Kalamazoo (Michigan) Public Schools, and Miss Marion C. Andros, Supervisor of Art, Kalamazoo (Michigan) Public Schools.

The author would also like to thank the following people for supplying photographs which appear in this book: Mr. John F. Agee, Los Alamos, New Mexico; and Mr. John C. Vitale, Art Instructor at Harvey High School, Painesville, Ohio.

Third Printing, 1974
Copyright © 1969 by Sterling Publishing Co., Inc.
419 Park Avenue South, New York, N.Y. 10016
Distributed in Canada by Saunders of Toronto, Ltd., Don Mills, Ontario
British edition published by Oak Tree Press Co., Ltd., Nassau, Bahamas
Distributed in Australia and New Zealand by Oak Tree Press Co., Ltd.,
P.O. Box J34, Brickfield Hill, Sydney 2000, N.S.W.
Distributed in the United Kingdom and elsewhere in the British Commonwealth
by Ward Lock Ltd., 116 Baker Street, London W 1
Manufactured in the United States of America
All rights reserved
Library of Congress Catalog Card No.: 69–19486
Sterling ISBN 0–8069–5122 –2 Trade   Oak Tree 7061–2210 0
5123 – 0 Library

⫸ ⫸ ⫸ CONTENTS ⫷ ⫷ ⫷

Illus. 1. A crayon mosaic. The tesserae are cut in varying shapes from paper that has been rubbed with crayon. The bits are then inlaid on a previously composed pattern drawn on a stiff board. Contrast in color values is the key to a pleasing crayon mosaic. See Chapter 5, page 51.

Illus. 2. Another type of mosaic. This is composed of melted wax crayons, kept less than 1/8 of an inch thick, poured onto tin foil to harden. The solidified, broken layers are glued to paper. India ink and pen were used for the lines that further define the basic shapes.

Preface

The crayon's full potential is seldom realized. While it is without doubt the most popular art tool within the school classroom and home, most people fail to appreciate its versatility. It is inexpensive, always accessible, colorful, and "messless"—but did you realize that there are numerous techniques for using the crayon? Have you experimented with all of the methods shown in this book?

The purpose of this volume, then, is to offer a multitude of techniques and inspiring ideas, to provide a background for those interested in exploring with crayons. The book is intended to serve as a guide for classroom teachers. But its usefulness will go beyond the school. The parent and home hobbyist, those active in recreational programs of a diverse nature—scouting work and church activities—will also find practical ideas to follow in the text and as they view the many exciting illustrations collected here.

Some of the techniques are very simple to execute and are suitable for children of nursery school and primary grades. Other techniques require a more complex system of planning and execution, and are best suited for older children and adults. There are crayon techniques in the book to challenge the creative talents of everyone—regardless of age, level of development or range of previous artistic experience.

The author, Professor Alkema, has for many years motivated both children and adults to explore the many possibilities for using crayons. His diverse experiences within the classroom have been captured by the camera for this book, and show what students of different ages are capable of. Frequently, he provides valuable suggestions aimed directly at the classroom teacher. The parent and home hobbyist may look upon this book as a teacher-substitute, not only to learn from, but to teach from, and to motivate others to explore, invent and create with crayons on their own.

THE EDITORS

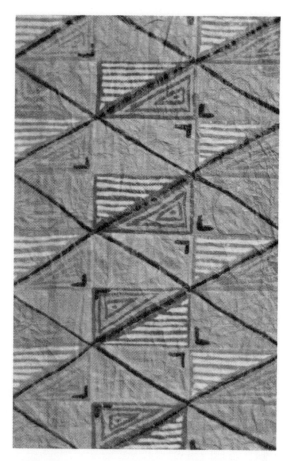

Illus. 3. Crayon on crushed paper bag. One is not confined to smooth paper surfaces in crayon work—sandpaper and brown paper bags, for example, give texture that cannot be achieved in other ways. Here, an Indian pattern composed entirely in line seems to have been painted on leather.

Illus. 4. An oil pastel creation. The effects of an oil painting can be achieved without paints simply by brushing turpentine lightly onto a drawing made with oil pastels. This softens and blends the bright crayon hues. Afterwards, the shapes can be outlined with pen and India ink.

Oil pastels are preferred for outdoor drawing excursions as they are dustless and the colors set within 48 hours. Watercolor washes and liquid starch may be effectively used in conjunction with oil pastels, instead of turpentine.

Crayon art with oil sticks on textured paper will create rough lines, as in Illus. 5. Again a turpentine wash can be used to soften the lines.

What's Available in Crayons?

Of all media used in the school art curriculum, crayons are perhaps the most popular. Available in a wide variety of hues including silver, gold and flesh tones, crayons are inexpensive, accessible and available in a wide selection of sizes and shapes. The physical appearance of crayons differs from thick to thin, round to octagon, to meet the needs of students from nursery age to adult level. You may also obtain flat-sided crayons, made so as not to roll across a slanted table or desk top.

There was a time when the wax crayon was almost the only type in production and in use. But not so today. The ingredients of crayons vary, allowing the artist to produce a variety of interesting effects. Dull, pastel and transparent effects are achieved with some crayons, while waxy, shiny, enamel-like surfaces are created with other types. Some crayons suggest the rich surfaces of an oil painting. Others are water-soluble, and produce effects difficult to distinguish from a watercolor painting. Types of crayons the inquiring artist can explore include fluorescent, chalk pastel, oil pastel, oil, pressed, water crayons, pencil crayons and wax crayons.

Oil Pastels

The oil pastel crayons, manufactured or distributed under different trade names, are oil-base crayons with many unique properties which distinguish them from the usual wax crayon. A combination of crayon and pastel, they have the cleanliness of crayons and the intensity and exceptionally brilliant colors of pastels.

They may be applied to paper with a smooth, even texture not achieved with other types of crayon. Oil

Illus. 6. In blending oil pastels, avoid random movements and use parallel strokes all in the same direction. Oil pastels will cover such surfaces as brick, cloth and cork.

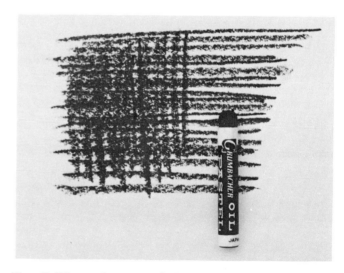

Illus. 7. When a large area is to be colored smoothly, it is most important to avoid random strokes. Aim for a layer of uniform thickness. Use your fingertip, a wad of cotton or a facial tissue for final smoothing.

Illus. 8. To scratch lines and patterns in solid areas of color use a knife or a single-edge razor blade (safety type) and be careful.

pastels may be easily blended by placing one color on top of another contrasting color, and by rubbing the two colors with facial tissue, a wad of cotton, or your fingertip. The oil base of these crayons eliminates all dust, no matter how heavily the colors are applied. Within 48 hours, the colors of a drawing will set, making the use of a fixative unnecessary. An impasto can be created by building colors one upon another, just as thick oils or acrylics are applied with a palette knife. Oil pastels may be applied to many kinds of surfaces—including brick, wood, cardboard, canvas, tagboard, cloth, cork and cement. Oil pastels are excellent for quick, on-the-spot sketches, and are easy to carry along on a sketching excursion when drawing from nature.

The range of available colors is indeed wide. Boxes containing as many as 50 different hues are available. You actually need not mix colors since almost any desired hue is commercially available. However, unusual and beautiful hues may be obtained by mixing and blending two colors together. When mixing or blending, do not apply color at random; that is, in uneven, diffused strokes. The first color should be spread in one direction, in parallel, close, evenly spaced strokes. The second color may then be applied over the first, again using parallel strokes which move in the same direction. Finally, the color which was applied first is now used again, over the first two layers of color. The last layer (also stroked in the same direction) serves to blend the two colors together. (See Illus. 6.)

Random strokes of the oil pastel should also be avoided when a large area is to be smoothly colored. The crayon should be applied in close, parallel strokes. Then, the same crayon should be applied again, but now running in the opposite direction, creating a cross-hatch effect with close parallel strokes. A second application of crayon should be used to fill in any openings that reveal the background paper. (See Illus. 7.)

A knife blade or safety-edged razor blade may be effectively used in conjunction with the oil pastel crayons. Lines may be scratched through the solid oil pastel crayoned areas to produce patterns and the illusion of texture. (See Illus. 8.) Scratched lines, applied to the colored trunk of a tree, for example, would serve to further suggest the texture of the tree. Brick patterns of a house might be scratched through the solid tone provided by the oil pastel. And the knife or razor blade is most effective in correcting color errors. Oil pastels may be scraped away so that a new and different color may be applied.

A facial tissue is a handy tool for use with oil pastels, not only for blending colors together by rubbing, but also for keeping colors clean. The pointed end of an oil pastel should be wiped often with facial tissue, as the crayon will absorb some of the last color it was used upon. Repeated wiping keeps the color pure.

Oil pastels may effectively be mixed with other media. Turpentine may be painted over oil pastels to produce interesting oil washes and to simulate the effect of an oil painting. When turpentine is applied too heavily, it will lift the color from the base, so it must be brushed on lightly as a thin wash. Turpentine will also dissolve oil

Illus. 9. Muted yellow, brown and green tones of oil pastel were applied to tagboard to create the violin, leaves and soft background. Turpentine, applied with a brush, softened and blended the colors still further. Brush marks are visible—leave them in, as they help to simulate an oil painting.

Illus. 10. This geometric design was created on corrugated cardboard with oil pastels. A thin coat of turpentine, brushed on, softened the color areas slightly.

Illus. 11. To suggest the character of a tempera painting, turpentine was "blended" with oil pastels to create these flat tones of muted gray, coral, blue and bright green. In this case, the "dip and draw" technique was used. The crayons were dipped in the turpentine, applied to the paper, then dipped again, continuously.

pastels. However, it is fine to soften harsh lines and color areas, and to blend colors. Through experimentation, you will achieve many unusual effects through the use of turpentine. (See Illus. 4, 9 and 10.)

The "dip and draw" approach to using oil pastels and turpentine will lead to some interesting results. Dip the pastel crayons in turpentine and proceed to draw. Continue to dip the pastel crayon as the pigment is removed from the pastel onto the paper. (See Illus. 11.)

Oil pastels may be used with watercolors or tempera paint. Since oil pastels are water-resistant, watercolor or tempera washes will cover the uncrayoned portions of the paper without affecting the oil pastel colors. The resulting resist technique may be used to produce some fine contrasts in color and texture.

Liquid starch may also be used with oil pastels. Soak absorbent paper in liquid starch and be prepared for some amazing results when you apply oil pastels.

Oil pastels set after about 48 hours. However, if your drawing is to be stored for some time, place a thin sheet of plastic, acetate or wax paper over the art work before rolling it.

For applying oil pastels to textiles, use either of two methods. In the first method, draw with oil pastels directly upon the cloth. Exert pressure on the crayon so that vivid lines and colors are achieved. "Set" the colors by placing the textile between two sheets of newspaper, one dampened and one dry. Press the dampened sheet with a warm iron.

In using the second method, melt a piece of oil pastel in a small container and add an equal amount of picture varnish. Apply the resulting paint on the cloth with a brush. The medium may be thinned by adding varnish.

Oil pastels may also be used to stain a piece of natural wood. Apply the desired color and then wipe the wood with a turpentine-soaked cloth. Rich, waxy crayon colors will bring a dull piece of wood to life.

An excellent medium for the artist who wants to handle a minimum of materials during an outdoor sketching trip, oil pastels require no messy palette, brushes or mixing tools, easel or canvas. You work without waste or dried-out colors, for oil pastels may be applied dry. The turpentine may be applied later, to achieve simulated oil painting effects.

Illus. 12. The proper method of spatter painting with water crayons.

Water Crayons

Water-soluble crayons have been added to the crayon family in the last few years and provide another interesting medium for the experimenting artist. Water crayons, which are available in stick form, may be used in a variety of ways. You can sketch dry on dry paper to achieve crayon and chalk pastel effects. Blend the sketch with a wet brush to produce striking watercolor and tempera-like effects.

Try applying dry water crayons to water-soaked paper to create brilliant, bold line drawings. Or, dip the water crayon in water and apply it to dry paper. Whenever you apply a wet brush to a dry water crayon, it picks up the colored pigment of the crayon. When the liquid from the brush is then applied to paper, it takes on the appearance of watercolor. The direct approach is to dissolve some of the crayon in a water tray to provide a watercolor medium.

Water crayons may effectively be used in conjunction with a spatter-painting technique. Place some shapes cut or torn from paper or cardboard upon a sheet of background paper. Leave them loose or tip them on with rubber cement. Or find interesting ferns, weeds and flowers from nature and arrange them artistically on your background paper. Next, draw an old wet toothbrush slowly across a stick of water crayon to create a fine mist of paint. The spattered specks of paint will fall upon the shapes and background paper. Since the paint will fly in all directions, hold the toothbrush with bristles down close to the paper. Allow the paper to dry, once enough paint has been spattered upon the surface. When it is dry, remove the cut shapes or nature's forms and observe their silhouette as seen upon the background paper. Choose a light-color water crayon if the background paper is dark in value, and a dark water crayon to show up best on a light sheet of paper. Strong contrasts of color will allow an observer to differentiate the shapes better when the painting or poster is seen at a distance. (See Illus. 12 and 13.)

Interesting effects may be achieved when crayon media are mixed. Oil pastels and water crayons may be used together, for example, in a single composition on heavy watercolor paper. Using the water-soaked crayon approach, paint in the light soft areas. Shadows and dark, strong areas may be intensified by adding oil pastel

Illus. 13. This spatter painting was created by a 4-year-old in nursery school.

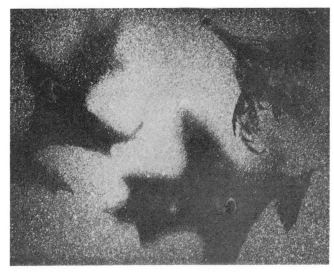

crayon to the water crayon scene. And finally, a turpentine-soaked brush touched over the shadows and dark spots will enrich the heavy areas.

Fluorescent Crayons

Water crayons and fluorescent pastels can be combined to produce unusual color combinations, as in Illus. 14. Buildings and their details were first painted with dissolved water crayon. The highlights were then added with fluorescent pastels. The gray, subdued paper and the

Illus. 14. "City Street," a painting owned by the American Crayon Co., was made with dissolved water crayons, and highlights were added with fluorescent pastel crayons (pinks and blues).

Illus. 15. In "Portrait of a Woman," also owned by the American Crayon Co., the features were outlined in black crayon and then fluorescent crayons were used for all the rest of the work. However, the fluorescents have been applied lightly and with good taste.

dull tones of the water crayon are sparked up by the contrasting, intense fluorescent areas.

Fluorescent crayons are the brightest crayons made. Their intensity may be a bit overwhelming if all colors within a composition are fluorescent in nature. They are best used to produce exciting highlights in drawings or paintings which have been dominantly colored with less intense crayons, such as oil pastels, water crayons or wax crayons. But for lecture use, where the speaker is at a distance from his audience, use of fluorescent crayons exclusively is highly recommended. The colors become blazing when viewed under a "black light."

The "Portrait of a Woman" in Illus. 15 was first outlined with black crayon and finished with fluorescent crayons. The intense fluorescent colors have been sparingly applied, allowing the dull green background paper to become an important part of the design. The dull paper and the intense fluorescent colors complement each other quite effectively. A bright colored paper used with the bright fluorescent color would have created an overwhelmingly gaudy effect.

Crayon Pencils

In crayon pencils the crayon "lead" is surrounded by wood, and it can be sharpened as a pencil. Although it is a good drawing tool, the colors appear rather dull and lifeless when applied to paper. To get more intense color, the pencil point must be dipped into water before applying it to paper. The crayon pencil may be effectively used in executing a graph paper design, a technique described in Chapter Six.

Chalk Pastel Crayons

Chalk pastel crayons are an exciting medium to experiment with because their colors are so intense and the brilliant hues are so responsive and smooth when applied to paper. Chalk pastels produce a soft, velvety texture that invites you to produce broad, sweeping strokes. You are thus able to express yourself freely. Although chalk pastels are not recommended for use on the blackboard,

Illus. 16. Drawing with a white chalk pastel on a black rough-surfaced paper, the artist was able to create these broad, shaded strokes and create a simple but effective work for the American Crayon Co.

they will adhere beautifully to many kinds of paper, and also to cloth. The highly pigmented chalk pastels are especially useful for making posters and murals of bright designs.

Most brands of chalk pastel are available as square sticks, so they can be used on their sides to create broad sweeps of shaded color. Also, square pastels will not roll.

Illus. 16 shows one interesting effect that can be achieved. A white chalk pastel was applied to a rough

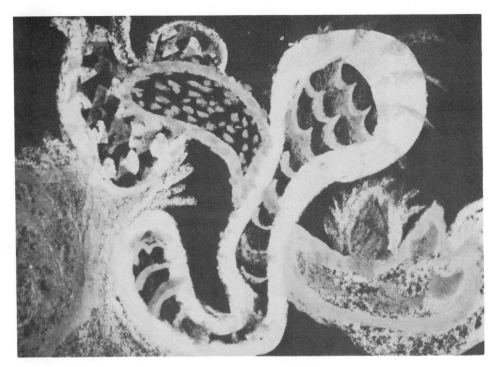

Illus. 17. Chalk pastel crayons dipped in liquid starch were used here to produce brilliant flowing effects and a full range of tones on black construction paper. The colors used were blue, purple and cream.

textured sheet of black paper. A few simple strokes seem to say much in this drawing. The square shape of the pastel enabled the artist to use broad, shaded strokes.

Chalk pastels may be effectively combined with other media. Unusual textured effects, for example, may be obtained when chalk pastels are used with water and liquid starch. The pastel stick should first be dipped in water and then into a pan of liquid laundry starch. When you apply this water-and-starch-dampened stick to paper, you get exciting rich tones. The liquid starch acts as a fixative so that drawings need not be sprayed later. (See Illus. 17.)

When used in combination with white powdered tempera paint, chalk pastels produce some unusual results. First soak a sheet of absorbent background paper, such as manila, in water. Shake about one teaspoon of powdered tempera paint over the water-soaked paper. Using a brush, blend the water and powder paint over the whole surface of the paper. Using the side of your chalk pastels, now draw line designs into the white surface while the

powder paint is still wet. You will produce breathtaking results! The powdered paint acts as a fixative so the pastel hues will not rub off.

Sugar water provides yet another interesting medium for use with chalk pastels. Sweeten some water and place it in a large flat pan. Soak a sheet of absorbent paper, such as manila, in this solution and place the watered sheet on dry sheets of newspaper. Apply designs in chalk pastel to the wet surface. Colors appear much more vibrant and intense when applied this way to the water-soaked paper. The sugar acts as a fixative.

The heavily textured painting in Illus. 18 was created with "freart," a chalk pastel. The procedure was as follows: One part of granulated sugar was mixed with four parts of water in a waterproof container. Sticks of "freart" pastels were dipped into this mixture and then applied directly to the paper's surface. The painting displays a live-color effect which needs no further fixing. When you use this procedure, your finished pieces will

dry quickly. You can safely display or store them without fear of smudging.

Background papers may also be painted with buttermilk in preparation for the application of chalk pastel lines and shadings. Buttermilk enables you to blend chalk colors in an effective manner and serves as a fixative too. Black construction paper painted either with buttermilk or sugar water provides the background you need to make chalk pastel colors appear their richest and most striking against a contrasting surface.

Chalk pastels produce particularly beautiful results when used with the crayon stencil technique described in Chapter Four.

Commercial hair sprays provide a suitable fixative for chalk pastel drawings on dry paper. Facial tissues or cloth are handy for softening and blending chalk pastel colors.

Wax Crayons

Of all available crayons, the wax crayon, of course, remains the most popular type as far as the elementary school classroom is concerned. All illustrations in this book, unless indicated otherwise, were created with wax crayons. But it should immediately be pointed out that many of the techniques suggested for use with wax crayons can also be effectively executed with the other types of crayons.

For Illus. 19, a drawing with wax crayons, a rough-textured surface (pebbled cardboard) was chosen. The idea was to show the isolated little house on the edge of a river and its reflection in the water with as few strokes as possible. The sketch was successful because the pebbled face kept the soft blend of wax colors high on the surface of the cardboard.

Experimentation, the Road to Knowledge

Experiment with the many different available kinds of crayon to determine which tool will allow you the most effective expression of your personal ideas. Water crayons may inspire a great amount of interest in one artist, but may prove frustrating to another. Fluorescent crayons may attract your eye, while another artist might

Illus. 19. Wax crayon drawing made for the American Crayon Co. on a pebbled surface cardboard. The rough effect is nevertheless soft in feeling.

prefer the more subdued hues provided by wax crayons. Experience with all types of crayons is the best teacher.

When exploring with the various types of crayon, you can easily fall into the trap of repetition. You like one type of crayon and one type of drawing and you stick with it. All well and good. But you will avoid repetition if you discover different methods of handling the crayon. Explore consistently and you will discover and invent new ways for expressing your ideas. Many different effects can be achieved with the crayon. Try for them. Variety in expression adds spice to life and is an indication of an artist's continued creative and mental growth.

How might a classroom teacher encourage students to explore the use of the crayon? How might the weekend artist and home hobbyist use this tool? What varieties of method and technique are worth investigating and trying? The rest of the chapters explore and demonstrate many answers to these vital questions.

CHAPTER TWO

Exploring with the Crayon's Point, Peeled Side, and Blunt End

Line Drawing

The point of the crayon is especially suited for making lines. Experimentation with line drawings increases your awareness of the beauty of line and helps you execute a variety of line effects, any one of which might be chosen to portray a specific idea. Answering the question, "What kind of lines can *you* make with the point of your crayon?" will bring forth in any group numerous attempts leading to new ideas, discoveries and observations.

Illus. 20. Following a discussion about the nature of lines, Rodney, a sixth-grade student, used the point of his crayon to draw this "Spring Floral Arrangement," a stylized still life.

"Lines can be short and they can be long. They can curve. Sometimes they curve quickly, at other times slowly. Some lines are straight or angular, having sharp points and corners. Others are wavy, zigzagged and scalloped." These are the answers you are likely to get from a class of young students. The artist's problem is to determine what lines best interpret certain objects from nature. Some objects lend themselves to jagged lines, the edges of a leaf, for example, and lightning during a storm.

Illus. 21. A fifth-grade student was inspired by discussion of line to show these 6 effects (top left to lower right): straight and skipping, straight and continuous, slow curving, fast curving, zigzag, and scalloped.

17

Illus. 22. Marie, another sixth-grader, used the same flower-and-pot model as Rodney, but created a very different interpretation.

Scalloped lines, of course, indicate the waves of an ocean.

Questions concerning the nature of lines and their use encourage even the youngest artists to think and to make their own observations. Children often get the wonderful feeling that they, themselves, are making certain discoveries. A demonstration displaying types of lines would deprive students of this self-searching and exploration. However, after the students have run out of ideas, a demonstration might be initiated in a class to suggest ideas that have been overlooked.

Illus. 20 through 24 reveal the many diverse ideas which come forth when the characteristics of line are discussed by a group and given consideration.

In the spring of the year various pots and bouquets of flowers were set around a sixth-grade room for inspiration during a crayon drawing experience. After a discussion involving the use of line, one sixth-grader used pure line to convey his subject—flowers within a bowl—as seen in Illus. 20.

Another student used line in quite a different way in interpreting the same subject. In Illus. 22, the lines do more than just serve as pure line. They create shapes. And these resulting shapes are colored in with solid colors, sometimes heavily applied and sometimes lightly applied so as to create an interesting variety in texture and value. The imaginative background is also composed of shapes that are colored in, but they unite rather than conflict with the major subjects. Later we shall see how further discussion inspired other sixth-graders to use crayon in interpreting the spring floral arrangement.

On one occasion, fifth-grade students were asked to imagine what they might see through a microscope, and to portray their imaginary, magnified views of nature on paper, using crayon. In Illus. 23, the artist drew many kinds of lines to depict crawling germs and gremlins. He surrounded them with interesting line patterns that helped to tie the various creeping creatures with the other parts of the design.

In Illus. 24, the artist preferred a non-representational line design, which does not reveal any object recognizably. The beauty of curved lines is excitingly portrayed in this drawing. Lines rhythmically flow in a curved and countercurved movement, causing the eye to bounce about from one area to another. Rich, dark reds,

Illus. 23. When asked to draw what he might see through a microscope, John, a fifth-grade student, used the point of his crayon to create lines and shapes, not only of protozoa, but of gremlins and even bunnies. The amusing feeling comes from the combination of bright colors with the wriggly shapes.

blues and purples are contrasted with gleaming, narrow areas of the white background paper which come peeking through and which also suggest the nature of line.

Illus. 24. Given the same theme, René imagined non-representational curves and countercurves in orderly profusion. The free flowing crayon lines create a rhythm.

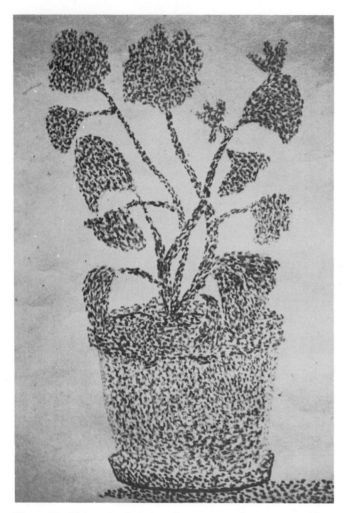

Illus. 25. Using just dots of crayon color—green, blue, red and orange—James created a "Spring Floral Arrangement" in Pointillistic style reminiscent of Seurat.

Dot Pictures (Pointillism)

In experimenting further you will discover that the pointed end of the crayon is useful in making circles and dots. These can be small or large, elongated, fully round or oval. Dots can be carefully drawn or rendered quickly by using small, short touches which together produce an even or softly graded tone—a stippled effect. Try making a picture by using just dots to portray your idea.

If you have a chance, go to a museum (or look in an art book) and examine carefully a painting by the French post-Impressionist painter, Georges Seurat. Seurat did not use crayons in executing his paintings, but his method of applying paint may be adapted to our use of the crayon. Seurat never mixed his colors to create new hues: he did not mix yellow with blue when he wanted green. Instead, he interspersed many small dots of yellow paint with numerous dots of blue paint, and the eye of the beholder naturally fused the many dots together to form the color green. The dots of color in Seurat's paintings are small and close together, and his greens appear as greens until you look closely to see that many small specks of color were applied in mosaic-like fashion.

In using crayon, you may not wish to place blue side by side with yellow dots to create green—or yellow next to red to produce orange—since you have the colors green and orange in your box of crayons. However, your drawings would be most interesting if you applied your crayon as Seurat applied paint. This technique is called *Pointillism*, a most appropriate title since the many dots of color appear as sharp points.

After viewing reproductions of Seurat's paintings, one of my sixth-grade students decided to use Pointillism in executing his Spring Floral Arrangement. Illus. 25 reveals how this technique affected the whole style of the crayon drawing. Precise dots of color applied in mosaic-like fashion make up the entire picture.

The Dutch master Vincent Van Gogh painted in a style which made use of *elongated* dots or streaks of color. Van Gogh's painting "Starry Night" (and numerous other of his paintings which you will find in art books) reveal how dots of color may change their shape so as to achieve a certain style. Van Gogh's style might also be adapted to your application of crayon.

Illus. 26 reveals four preliminary practice drawings created by one student. The top left example demonstrates that dots can be oval in shape and can vary in size from small to large. The top right example reveals circular dots, most of which are hollow in the center. At the lower left, our young artist has deliberately broken off the sharp point of his crayon so that an interesting

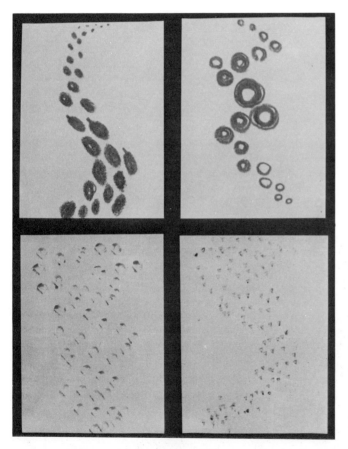

Illus. 26. Experiments with the point of the crayon in making dots. In the lower examples, the tip of the crayon has been broken off to get the irregular shapes.

jagged pattern might be rendered as a result of stippling. At the lower right, a triangular-shaped pattern resulted when the crayon's point was rapidly jabbed onto the paper's surface.

There are other ways to make dot patterns. See if you can produce a drawing which consists completely of dots, much as Seurat or Van Gogh would have done it.

Combining Lines, Dots and Circles

Now it might be fun to make a drawing which combines both lines and dots. Illus. 27 reveals a line-and-dot arrangement which suggests a Pennsylvania Dutch design. There is a wonderful sense of variety in this drawing— lines are straight, angular and curved; dots are circular, oval and elongated. Variety in the repetition of elements lends this design interest.

Perhaps you would like to create a non-representational design which combines dots, circles and lines. The elements might run from one end of your paper to the other in a vertical or horizontal movement. Try making overlapping lines, or lines which appear to cross over or under other lines. In what manner can you join your circles together? Your circles' edges might touch or overlap, or lines might join them together.

In Illus. 28 note that strong zigzag lines, circles and patterns are combined to create a stylized drawing of an underwater scene. Observe the many different circle, dot and line patterns which decorate the fish and their marine environment.

Representational Drawings

Obviously, the point of the crayon is most fittingly used for drawing representational pictures. Primary-grade pupils (and older) love to create recognizable images associated with their local environment. Pets, friends, teacher, and parents are most frequently depicted in their crayon drawings.

The young student should be encouraged to show contrast in as many ways as possible. There are three major considerations: First, thought should be given to

Illus. 27. Employing a combination of crayon lines, dots and circles, Ralph, a fifth-grader created what resembles a Pennsylvania Dutch pattern.

Illus. 28. In this stylistic version of an underwater scene, zigzag is the predominant pattern, but it is nicely combined with circular bubbles and oval dots of crayon color. Note how the fishes' scales seem to overlap through clever use of zigzagging colors on the dark background.

contrasts in color *value*. "Which crayon colors will show up best if light-colored background paper is used?" Perhaps the student should use both light and dark colors in a single composition. "Which colors will appear most vivid against dark paper?"

Secondly, thought should be given to contrasts in the *intensity* of colors. Solid *dull* areas of gray, brown and certain shades of green and blue will beautifully complement the fiery, stimulating, *brilliant* areas of red, yellow and orange. High and low intensity colors should be juxtaposed harmoniously.

And third, contrasts in the *texture* of the applied crayon, to lend added interest, can be easily achieved by varying the pressure exerted upon the crayon. Pressing hard on the crayon's point creates thick, wax-filled, shiny, rich impastos; pressing lightly allows for a soft, light, delicate effect.

Manila paper is an ideal surface for crayon drawings because its rough, toothy surface permits a wide range of textural surfaces when the pressure applied to the crayon is varied. The combination of the two textural extremes is most exciting to behold in a single composition.

Illus. 29 through 33 reveal the interests of children as expressed in their crayon drawings. Also, the drawings demonstrate the young child's ability to achieve a variety of effects with the crayon's point. In Illus. 29 the crayon has been both heavily and lightly applied. The garments of the figure in red are rich with wax, heavily applied. The garments of the remaining two important figures are more lightly colored and offer a textural contrast to the figure on the left and other areas within the composition. Note that small and large heavily-waxed areas are repeated and balanced throughout the design, as are the light, soft areas of crayon.

This drawing also displays the use of bright, intense reds, greens and touches of yellow. These glowing colors afford a pleasant contrast next to the dull blues and grays.

Children should be encouraged to view their crayon drawings from a distance to determine if their forms can be seen from afar. It may be necessary for them to press

Illus. 29. "Two Ladies Under an Umbrella" is the work of a third-grade student in a Kalamazoo, Michigan, public school.

more heavily upon their crayons to achieve bolder compositions.

Illus. 30. "The Tree House" by a Kalamazoo fourth-grader shows how crayon is heavily applied throughout a drawing to tagboard, a shiny surface. Although textural contrasts are lacking, the artist gets good contrast from light and dark values and intensities—bright reds and yellows next to the brown tree, the dull blue sky and the dark house.

Illus. 31. In this drawing by a second-grade student in Kalamazoo, the large shapes have been colored with light strokes, revealing much of the manila paper's texture. The rich black line affords a much needed color contrast and helps to define the picture's many shapes.

Illus. 32. A fourth-grader in Kalamazoo entitled her drawing on manila paper, "Hurrying Home in the Storm." The light-textured lawn and sidewalk make the heavily-waxed, intensely colored figures stand out. Slanting the figures to suggest movement is a device usually learned at a later stage.

Illus. 33. "I Had Fun at the Fair" is a very complicated and busy work, filled with detail, surprisingly effective, and—even more astonishing—it was drawn by a second-grade student in the Kalamazoo public schools. All crayoned areas are rather timidly applied, but a dark outline does wonders in defining and distinguishing the many separate forms and shapes.

The Peeled Side:
Shading and Blending

You can achieve interesting effects by peeling one side of a wax crayon and lightly sliding it over paper. Large areas become rapidly filled with delicate shades of color. Blending is easily performed if you put down the lightest shades first and gradually work the darker ones over and around them. In rendering a landscape, for example, the sky can be made to show subtle shades of blue, yellow and orange, instead of one monotonous color. Grassy areas can be made to display a combination of yellows, greens and blues, all softly blended to portray an earth of majestic beauty, possibly backed by misty mountains of purples, blues and tips of variegated white.

Colored construction paper (as in Illus. 34) provides a tone which can be used to unify all colors within a composition, and provide dramatic effect as well.

Children should be encouraged to create drawings which combine the flat strokes made by the crayon's peeled side with sharp, detailed and articulate lines created by the point of the crayon. Drawings take on added interest as sharp, bold, waxy, shiny lines combine with dull, flat, broad areas of delicate color.

"Imaginary Bird" (Illus. 35) by a 12-year-old mentally retarded student displays a fine example of how the crayon's peeled side has produced some lovely shades and blends of color. Applying the crayon in a light circular movement, the student created subtle greens, yellows, pinks, blues and browns to adorn the bird's wings and body feathers, as well as the lower background. The point of the crayon provided some contrasting, sharp lines and solid areas of color.

The practice drawings in Illus. 36 reveal some peeled crayon effects. At top left, the crayon was simply zigzagged back and forth before and after a notch had been cut with scissors in the peeled side. At top right, the larger circle was created by holding one end of the peeled crayon stationary while the other was swung completely around. The smaller circle was made by holding down the middle as the peeled crayon was swung around on its side. To create the bow shapes, the crayon was held in

Illus. 34. The peeled side of the wax crayon was used almost exclusively in this adult's rendering of a seascape on blue construction paper. Observe the softness of the waves and clouds. Back and forth movements of the peeled crayon established the green, blue and white waves, while circular movements of black crayon over the pink base color created the clouds. For shading and blending, the peeled side of a crayon is best. The crayon's point was used here to create the boats and to add highlights.

the middle and swung back and forth. In the middle left box, the cattails were created by rocking the blunt end of a crayon up and down. The blunt end was then pressed against the paper and twisted for the lower left example. At the lower right, ribbonlike lines were formed when the peeled crayon was swerved back and forth across the paper.

Illus. 35. "Imaginary Bird," the work of a mentally retarded 12-year-old, is a fine example of the soft shades and blends to be achieved with the peeled side of a crayon.

Illus. 36. Various effects you can obtain from a crayon's side and blunt end. Cutting a notch in the side is a trick that enables you to get flaglike stripes. The cross bows come from holding the crayon down in the middle and rotating it.

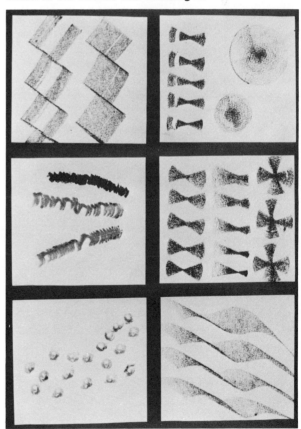

Illus. 37. A fifth-grader in the Parkview School, Wyoming, Michigan, using the side of her crayon to define the contours of her rabbit. At the same time the shading suggests the third dimension.

The side of the crayon is effective in establishing the contour of an object. If you press on one end of the crayon a bit more than on the opposite end, the crayon's side not only defines a shape but shades it in as well, thus suggesting the third dimension. Working in reverse order, you might shade in the background, leaving plain the positive shape of your subject which now moves forward into a frontal plane.

One of three types of shading (see Illus. 38) must be rendered consistently throughout a single composition. Always consider the source of your light.

In experimenting with the crayon's peeled side, you discovered that circles, for example, could be made by holding the crayon firm in the middle while turning it completely around on its side. Alternatively, the crayon can be held steady while the *paper* is turned with the other hand. You can make extra large circles by holding the crayon at one end, thus allowing the rest of the crayon to move in a circular path. Further experiments with a series of zigzag strokes will create patterns and

Illus. 38. Three methods of shading objects with the peeled side of a crayon. The light on the left ball is coming from the left, causing the right side to be engulfed in shadow. The middle ball has the light coming from the right. The light is shining head-on at the right ball, illuminating the front with a highlight and causing all the edges to darken.

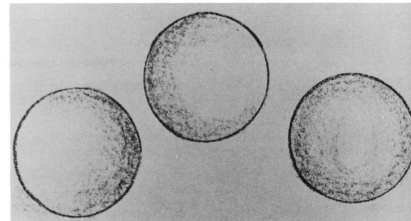

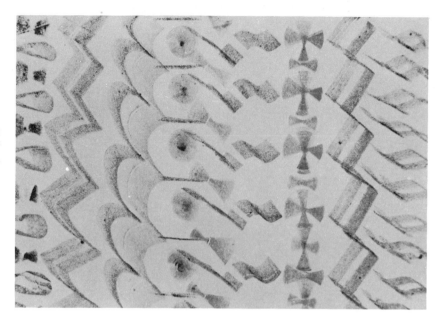

Illus. 39. To create a multitude of effects with the peeled side of a crayon was the aim of Doris, a fifth-grade pupil in this non-representational composition.

textures suggestive of brick, woven reed, roofing, shingles, etc.—very useful in drawing landscapes.

Following a discussion and period of experimentation, a fifth-grade student created the lovely geometric, non-representational design seen in Illus. 39. The side of the crayon was used exclusively to create the diversified patterns.

One classroom problem may occur with the peeling of crayons. Children are constantly taught at home and school to care for their property. The removal of a crayon's wrapping seems contrary to past training instructions, and the act seems to be a destructive one. Consequently, the teacher might ask for a donation of all old crayons at the conclusion of each school year, to be saved and used the following year. Crayons will readily be donated by students, whether whole or broken, and a large box of assorted colors can be quickly collected. When they peel old crayons, it will not seem to be so destructive.

Blunt End

Another useful part of the tool is the blunt end of the crayon. If you hold the crayon at a 45-degree angle, the flat ridge of the blunt end will produce a very narrow, controlled line. An interesting pattern of circular shapes develops as you explore. Press the flat end against your paper while giving the crayon a slight twist. Result: see lowest left box of Illus. 36. The crayon may purposely be broken so that the blunt end contains irregular, uneven edges, thus producing a different pattern as the crayon is pressed and twisted against the paper.

The crayon might be rocked back and forth as the blunt end is slowly pushed across the paper. A heavy zigzag line of thick wax is quickly established. (See middle left box of Illus. 36.) When might this line be used? What object might be created by using this technique? The formations might suggest stylized cattails, larkspurs or lilacs.

You will recall that three sixth-grade students ren-

dered spring floral arrangements in crayon when various bouquets were placed about the room. A fourth and far different technique for illustrating the same subject matter appears in Illus. 40. After experimenting with the crayon's peeled side and blunt end, this sixth-grade student used these two parts of the crayon exclusively in interpreting the subject. Study the example and see if you can determine which part of the crayon—the side, or the blunt end—was used to make the basket, flowers and leaves.

How interesting crayon drawings become as you experiment and as your inner ideas, thoughts and feelings unfold and are portrayed!

Illus. 40. Beatrice, another sixth-grade student, interpreted the spring flower arrangement by using the newly-found full potential of her crayon—its peeled side and blunt end. She rocked the crayon back and forth, twisted it on its end and side, and rubbed it every which way over the paper to create this lovely still-life.

CHAPTER THREE

Exploring with Design

The Art Elements

An artist uses a number of elements when expressing ideas. *Line*, for example, is an element usually used to describe *form*, to create a *shape*. And *space*, real or illusionary, is an important element in the art product. Sometimes an artist is interested only in two-dimensional space, that is, the height and width of an object, but more often with three-dimensional space, the height, width and depth of an art object.

The elements of *texture* or *pattern* are used mostly to convey the "feel" of a shape, area or object. If crayon is heavily and roughly applied, the texture is said to be rough. If crayon is lightly applied to shiny paper, the texture is seen as smooth. Sometimes the artist will create a pattern to give the illusion of a certain desired texture. For instance, a number of dark crayon dots, closely spaced on light paper, might suggest a rough area to the eye. But upon feeling the area, one discovers that the dark dots consist of lightly applied crayon, and are barely perceptible to the touch. Pattern often fools the eye. The truth comes out when the fingertips explore the area which the eye beholds.

Color is perhaps the most exciting element the artist can use to convey his idea, his feeling, his mood. A light color is of high value, a dark color is of low value. A very bright color is of a high intensity, whereas a dull color is low in intensity.

Colors have certain characteristics which make them fun to use. For example, they suggest warmth and coolness. Colors associated with sources of heat, such as fire or the sun, suggest warmth. Red, yellow and orange give you a warm feeling. Colors associated with cool aspects of nature, such as the sky, the ocean and the mountains, suggest coolness. Blue is a cool color. This is

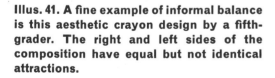

Illus. 41. A fine example of informal balance is this aesthetic crayon design by a fifth-grader. The right and left sides of the composition have equal but not identical attractions.

Illus. 42. In this formally balanced design, the right and left sides are almost identical in the placement of the art elements. Drawn by an adult.

Illus. 43. The emphasis in this design by a fifth-grader is achieved by placing the central shapes against a plain dark background.

why so many theatre marquees announce the fact that they are air conditioned by having the letters "COOL" painted in blue.

Some colors seem to *advance*, while others appear to *recede*. When bright-colored and dull-colored crayons are applied to the same flat sheet of paper, the bright colors seem to come forward, whereas the dull colors cause the eye to move back into the distance. This illusionary advancement of color occurs in nature as well. Objects close to us are bright and intense. Distant hills, mountains and trees become pale and gray in color and dull in intensity.

Colors help to convey a mood. Red, yellow and orange are usually exciting to behold. They stimulate us. Some shades of green, blue and violet affect us as being somber and depressing. Reactions to color are highly personal and individual; people react slightly differently to certain colors. But, in general, a color is stimulating or restful, bright or dull, warm or cool, loud or quiet, striking or unobtrusive, to everyone.

In crayon compositions, an artist strives for contrast in every way possible: in lines that are long or short, slow curving or fast curving, angular or straight; in shapes that are large or small, with edges which are angular, curved or straight; in textures that are rough or smooth; in colors that are light or dark, bright or dull, cool or warm, striking or unobtrusive.

Principles of Aesthetic Crayon Design

The *arrangement* of the art elements—line, form, shape, pattern, texture, color—results in a design. What makes a design aesthetic and pleasing? It is not easy to make rules, for the moment a rule is established, some artist will violate it and do it quite successfully. However, reviewing certain principles of design may help you to create crayon drawings which are pleasing to the eye.

A crayon design does not seem right unless it displays *balance*. There must be equal weights or attractions on each side of the composition. In a design of formal balance, one half of the composition is the mirror image of the other. Objects from nature—a leaf or an apple blossom— have this formal balance. Crayon designs of informal balance have equal but not identical attractions on both sides of the composition, and this kind of balance is usually more interesting. It lures the observer to study the composition to see what makes the drawing balanced.

Illus. 42 provides an almost perfect example of formal balance. The two diamond shapes are almost identical on either side of the drawing's composition. (Identical hues fill the same corresponding shapes on the right and left hand sides.) Almost without exception, the line patterns surrounding the diamond shapes are placed in the same locations on either side. It is as if a design were painted on one side of a blotter and then folded so that the identical design is repeated on the opposite side.

In studying Illus. 41, an example of informal balance, you will note that no two circles are identical and all vary in size. The shapes and patterns, the attractions, are by no means identical when left and right sides of the composition are compared. Turn it upside down or sideways and the composition is still balanced. The greens, reds, oranges and blues do not fill corresponding shapes and locations, so they cause you to study the design to determine its balance. This is more interesting than the formally balanced design.

A design takes on added interest when it displays the principle of *continuity* or *rhythm*. This is achieved by repetition of the art elements: shape, color, texture, and line. But repetition must be handled carefully. If the elements are repeated in much the same way, the design may fade into the background. It may become monotonous.

Identical repetition is like the sound of a clock. Each tick is identical to the previous tick and future ticks. No one consciously listens to a clock—its sounds fade into the background. If the clock should suddenly utter sounds which are syncopated, you would sit up and listen because there would now be variety in the clock's repeated sounds.

You must show variety in the repetition of the elements of your crayon design if the composition is to be interesting. If a certain line is introduced, change this line somewhat when you repeat it within the design. If a certain color is introduced, lighten it or darken it just a

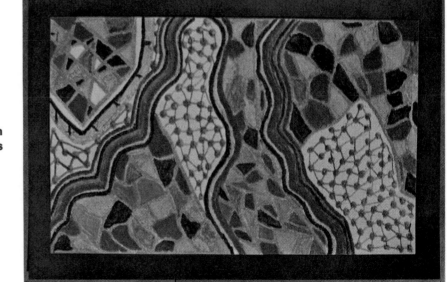

Illus. 44. Repetition of the art elements in this design by a fifth-grade student gives the work a rhythm.

Illus. 45. Slightly simpler is the repetition in this fifth-grader's design. Two large shapes, filled with multi-color line, offer focal points against odd-shaped areas of solid color.

little when it is repeated elsewhere. If many of the shapes within your design are small, introduce a few large ones so that your repeated shapes show variety. When a certain pattern is introduced, change the pattern in a subtle manner when it is repeated in another area. These subtle changes breathe new life into designs. They capture the eye of the beholder, as monotony dulls the eye.

A pleasing crayon design will reveal still another principle—*emphasis*. One part or related parts of a design must be more important than the surrounding areas. In other words, there must be a focal point, a center of interest. An artist must separate the essentials from the less important. All parts of a design should not scream out for the viewer's attention, nor should they be timidly rendered. There must be a contrast between the bold and modest areas of the composition, for the modest areas emphasize the bold, and vice versa.

Illus. 43 displays the principle of emphasis. The two large four-petalled shapes sing out as a focal point. The diagonal strip (orange and purple), which runs from one corner of the composition diagonally to the other,

likewise commands attention. The young artist has tastefully contrasted these busy areas with a quiet background of solids (greens, slate blue and pink). She has contrasted fussy areas with plain areas. Busy and plain areas complement each other, and the active parts of the design are emphasized by the very nature of this contrast.

The classroom teacher addressing 9-to-12-year-old children will find that the terms *balance*, *rhythm*, *emphasis* and *contrast* are sometimes beyond the students' comprehension. To make comments relative to design on the child's level of understanding, use the word "repeat." You might say, "I like the lines (or shapes, patterns or color) you have made. Where would you like to repeat them? Can you repeat them in a slightly different way? Do the parts of your crayon design look too empty? Too crowded? Does the design look right, feel right, to you? Which colors would you repeat (or change) to make your design show up best from a distance?" These questions do not dictate how the design is to be rendered, but they serve to activate the pupil into creating an aesthetic crayon design of his own invention.

Crayon Repeat Designs

Illus. 44 and 45, created by fifth-grade students, display a fine feeling for repetition of the design's various elements.

In Illus. 44, a mosaic-like pattern of dark blue, red, yellow, green and pink shapes, surrounded by an orange line, is repeated throughout the composition. A slow curving multi-colored band of lines defines some of the mosaic patterns and helps to tie the separate areas together. A lavender pattern of dots connected by thin lines offers a pleasing contrast to the rest of the composition. These repeated patterns seem to open up the otherwise solid design. They provide light areas in contrast to the darker mosaic patterns. The light delicate penetrable areas, on the other hand, are surrounded by heavy, massive bodies of rich impenetrable waxy mosaic-like islands. All colors, patterns and values are beautifully repeated and balanced, informally, throughout the rectangle. And the dark blue and orange border provides still another chance to repeat the design's chosen colors.

Illus. 45, a bit simpler in concept, consists mainly of solid shapes and defining lines and has no delicate, complicated contrasting pattern. The design has two fine, balanced focal points, however. Observe the two areas composed mainly of colored line, one near the upper left-hand corner and the balanced area near the lower right-hand corner. These two line-drawn shapes sing out against a background of solid color shapes.

Children will sometimes say, "I cannot draw" or "I cannot think of any patterns to make." Before the crayon-drawing experience begins, the classroom teacher should encourage children to view the many patterns in the clothes their friends are wearing. "Observe the dot patterns, star patterns and repeated shapes." Encourage children to close their eyes and imagine the many different interesting patterns they might create with crayon. "Perhaps oval shapes will float about, close to one another. Maybe you would like to connect these oval shapes with thin lines." Diamond shapes, triangular shapes, star formations, rectangles, squares, figure eights, circles, "x" formations—all can be suggested. "Will you place them close together? Will you repeat and balance your pattern elsewhere? Perhaps you would like to change your pattern just a little bit when it appears on the other side of your rectangle."

Use tight patterns with open patterns. Use dark colored patterns with light patterns. Many wonderful design creations will unfold as children's imaginations are activated through observation and discussion.

Geometric Repeat Designs

Older students (upper elementary grades and high school) as well as adults can consciously appreciate the rhythms of a repeat design that pulsates with life, and contains all the art elements: color, line, shape and texture.

Perhaps, as a beginning, you might wish to start with a simple geometric form, such as a circle, square or tri-

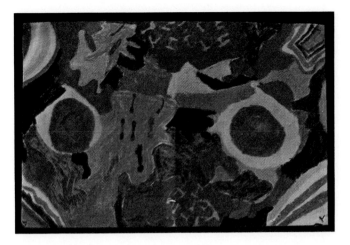

Illus. 46. A beginning project in design with a geometric form (the circle) turned into this when produced by a fourth-grader.

angle. Repeat the forms, overlap the forms, vary their size. Illus. 46 was created by a fourth-grade student to represent a design based on the circle. From circles within circles, short crayon strokes radiate out to create interesting patterns.

Designs on Folded Paper

A folded grid is a good form on which to start an artist of any age in planning, organizing and inventing rhythmic designs. You can fold the paper to any size in a variety of ways, to get creases or lines in all directions.

Working within the resulting rectangles, defined by the paper's creases, the artist can create rhythmic lines, shapes, patterns and colors and repeat those he likes. The success of the project is contingent upon the creative, imaginative abilities of the artist, and not upon the folding process. Experimentation is the key to success.

A grid of evenly spaced vertical and horizontal creases, running parallel to one another, were used for the designs seen in Illus. 47 through 51.

Illus. 47. Vertical and horizontal parallel creases in the paper aid the artist of any age in planning a geometric repeat design. This was the work of an adult.

The dark black areas of Illus. 47 present a bold design which contrasts with light, delicate rectangular diagonals and stripes.

A wheat stalk and decorative horizontal lines create a rhythmic pattern over the rectangular shapes defined by the paper's folds in Illus. 48.

Diagonal, purple crayon lines tie together the diamond shapes of Illus. 49 and serve to unify various elements of the total composition.

A black crayon boldly defines the horizontal, vertical and diagonal creases in Illus. 50. Observe how the many small rectangles are grouped together to form a large, light and dark checkerboard pattern. The combinations tend to simplify the design and divide it into an even number of prominent rectangles.

A ball-point pen was used to outline shapes confined by the parallel creases in Illus. 51. Many of the pencilled shapes were filled solid with crayon, whereas others were left uncolored and reveal the paper's surface.

Illus. 52 and 53 reveal that horizontal, vertical *and* diagonal creases can be combined within each sheet of paper to form a background for interesting designs.

Illus. 48. In this rectangular grid, a rhythmical pattern of wheat was the result of a project in repeat design.

Illus. 49. The thin diagonal lines tie the diamond shapes together in this grid design.

Illus. 50. Within each rectangle is a top right to lower left diagonal. These, crossing the vertical and horizontal lines, plus the alternating dark and light color values, combine the many small shapes into a checkerboard pattern.

Illus. 51. On the parallel creases, the adult artist drew open figure-eights, outlined them with a ball-point pen, and filled some in solid with crayon.

As the artist experiments with crayon on the folded grids, exciting, bold, geometric and rhythmic designs will emerge.

Illus. 52. A radial balance is evident here. All lines and shapes radiate from the middle of the design.

Scribble Repeat Designs

The scribble design approach is another effective means for introducing the beauty of repetition in design. With pencil or light crayon, draw overlapping lines at random without raising your pencil or crayon from the paper. Draw lines from one side of the sheet to the other and back again. Cross over previously made lines. Create vertical, horizontal and diagonal lines without lifting your pencil or crayon. At times run your pencil or crayon off the paper and then come back onto the paper. If lines run off the edge of the rectangle, the design becomes stabilized or anchored.

Now, look closely at your line design and see how you like it. Feel free to make changes in order to improve it. Do some of your shapes seem too similar in size? This can be monotonous. Erase a few lines or move them

Illus. 54. Flowing rhythmic lines characterize this scribble design in which the crayons were richly applied.

around so as to heighten the interest and appeal of the design. Do your shapes look as if they belong to each other? Do they get along well together? Perhaps you would like most of them to have curved edges or angular edges. Should a shape seem not to "belong" you can always make the necessary corrections. Play with the scribble until you have something you like.

Once the scribble line design is completed, you are ready to fill in some of the outlined shapes with solid color, and perhaps repeat some patterns. You can use different patterns to fill various-sized shapes defined by the scribble drawing. In contrast you might use solid, plain areas of color to fill a number of carefully chosen, balanced, repeated shapes.

The design in Illus. 54 is beautifully conceived. It represents a flowing rhythm established by ever-curving lines which sometimes run parallel to other lines, but frequently offer a countercurved movement. The design seems fixed, stable, monumental. Everything fits into place. One would not care to change a line or shape.

Illus. 53. Formal balance in a grid with horizontal, vertical and diagonal creases.

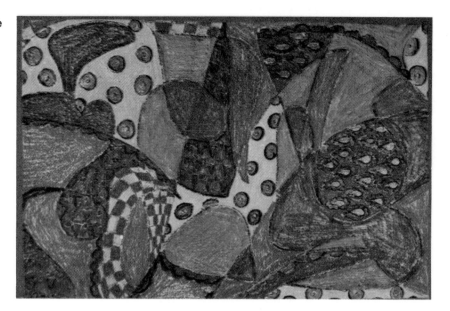

The colors and design of Illus. 55 are bold. The dominant warm red hues and contrasting cool blues cause the design to jump with excitement. The colors are heavily and richly applied. Observe how the polka-dot design changes in character as it is repeated from area to area. There is enough variety in the repetition of elements to avoid monotony.

The design pictured in Illus. 56 suggests a large bowl filled with flowers of delicate pattern. But since this is purely a non-representational design, the viewer is free to dream up his own interpretation. An exciting contrast is easily visible in the many patterns. Bold patterns, timid patterns, detailed patterns, open and uncomplicated patterns—all pulsate with life through juxtaposition.

Illus. 56. Recognizable objects can sometimes be found in a non-representational scribble design. Here one might imagine flowers overflowing a bowl.

Duplicated Name Designs

A unique and exciting approach to establishing repetition in elements of an aesthetic design is through the creation of a duplicated name design.

Fold a sheet of paper so that a central crease runs parallel with the paper's two longest sides. Using crayon, write your name or that of a friend large and legibly so the bottoms of the letters hit the fold of the paper. Press hard and make the name heavy. Fold the sheet on its axis the other way now and press the crayoned name hard against the clean paper. You will get a mirror image of your name. Go over this with crayon. Then fill in the loops of the letters and in between with little designs and details on both sides of the fold.

In Illus. 57, Michelle used her own name and decorated the many negative spaces and letter interiors with flowers, leaves and scrolled lines. When you stand the design upright (as printed) you cannot even see the writing. In fact, whenever a design is placed in a vertical direction, the name is difficult to distinguish. A name drawing should be artistic and nothing else. Keep it simple. You can use only a few curved lines in filling in, and restrict your use of bold patterns.

Sharon's name design is far more complicated (Illus. 58). In fact, her name can barely be distinguished even in normal writing position. A green and red checkerboard pattern solidly fills the two balanced shapes and offers a focal point. Other solid areas and open patterns serve to balance the design.

Line is the one element which characterizes and defines these name designs. If you have a name of few letters, you can add more linear shapes than with a complicated or intricate name. The heavy bold lines of a short name can afford a pleasing contrast against the lightly colored solid areas.

You might have eyes peek through one of the letters or add little cartoon touches. The most effective, however, are bright, warm colors embellishing a boldly written name in dark crayon. Name designs are fun to create. Make one based on your own name. Experiment with the name of a friend.

Illus. 57. This stately plant with its scroll and little flower decorations is actually constructed from a girl's name and its mirror image. Turn sideways to find Michelle.

Illus. 58. Sharon has added many details to disguise the pattern of her name.

CHAPTER FOUR

Exploring with Crayon Stencils

Non-Representational Designs

With the crayon stencil, the artist gains the use of a simple tool to repeat shapes within a design's composition, and obtain beauty in variety of repetition. The crayon stencil technique provides an excellent avenue by which the artist may realize the concept of repetition in design, of color, and of shape.

To begin, you will want to construct a stencil. Tagboard is the most suitable material as it does not tear easily under hard use.

An interesting shape, which we will call stencil A, is cut from the tagboard as pictured in Illus. 59. In planning your stencil's shape, try to think of something unusual and interesting, a shape which has irregular edges and protruding points. Geometric shapes such as the square, triangle, rectangle and circle appear frequently in art work, so try to avoid these. You might think of what happens to a square cookie when large and small bites are taken from its edges. An outlined shape, representing an imaginary, half-eaten cookie, might be just the shape needed to create an exciting stencilled repeat design.

With stencil A drawn on and cut from the tagboard, you are ready. Lay the stencil on a waste sheet, and apply crayon to the stencil's edges. (See Illus. 60.) Oil pastels, chalk pastels, fluorescent crayons, or wax crayons—all will do. Rub the crayon heavily along all the edges of the stencil's shape. Then place the crayoned stencil on a large sheet of background paper which will be the base for your final art. To get soft effects, you now rub or streak the crayon from the stencil's edges onto the background

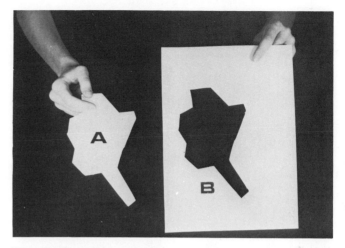

Illus. 59. To create a non-representational crayon stencil, cut an interesting shape from tagboard. Both stencils A and B can be used.

paper. Don't use crayon for this. Rub the crayon from the stencil, across the edge to the paper, using movements which always radiate away from the center of the cut stencil. A pencil eraser is an excellent tool for rubbing *wax* crayon from the stencil's edge. Your finger, facial

Illus. 60. Apply wax crayon, oil pastel, chalk pastel or fluorescent crayon around the edge of stencil A.

Illus. 61. Using your fingertip, rub the pastel crayon color from the edges of stencil A, onto the surface of your final background paper. Use strokes which radiate outward from the center of the stencil. (For wax-crayon rubbing, use a pencil eraser.)

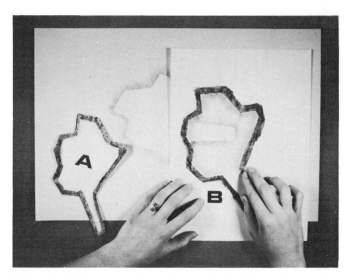

Illus. 63. Using your fingertip, radiate the crayon color onto your background paper. Use strokes which travel inward, toward the center of the removed stencil shape.

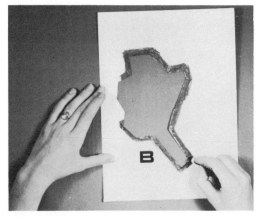

Illus. 62 (above). Next, apply crayon around the edges of the removed shape, Stencil B.

Illus. 64 (right). The finished design. By using both A and B, variety was achieved in the repeats. Overlapping the stencilled forms established small, interesting, accidental shapes which contribute to the variety.

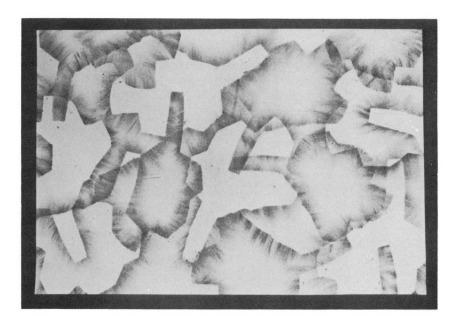

tissue or cotton wad may be used to stencil-rub chalk pastels, oil pastels or fluorescent crayons. (See Illus. 61.)

After all crayoned edges of stencil A have been rubbed onto the background paper, re-crayon the stencil along its edges and place it elsewhere on the paper. Rub it again, so the silhouette becomes visible at another area on the background paper. Try overlapping your stencilled design so that all parts appear related and united.

What now do you do with stencil B, the piece of tagboard from which stencil A was removed? Can this rectangular sheet of tagboard, containing the interesting hole in the middle, also be valuable? It certainly can. Rub crayon along the edges of the hole (see Illus. 62) and place it on the same background sheet. Now rub crayon inward from the edges of stencil B onto the background paper. You will notice that the resulting shapes are almost identical to those made with stencil A. However, the shapes made from B reveal streaks of color now radiating toward the center of the stencilled shape and not away from the center.

Variety comes from using both stencils A and B, and further variety is achieved when they are overlapped. New shapes are created sometimes by accident, while your thoughts are mainly with the placement of the large stencilled shapes. (See Illus. 64.) The new accidental shapes just have to correlate well with the surrounding shapes.

The crayon stencil technique provides a perfect opportunity for exploring the principle of good design: repetition, balance, continuity, rhythm and—another principle—unity of parts.

Consider your color scheme carefully. If black construction paper is to be your background, use light and preferably warm colors. Or reverse the values: use dark wax crayons, chalk pastels and oil pastels on light-colored paper. One good subtle color combination is obtained by using orange and yellow oil pastel on warm brown construction paper to give the feel of autumn.

A beautiful color combination is seen in Illus. 65. Ice cool light blue pastels have been stencilled onto a sheet of black construction paper.

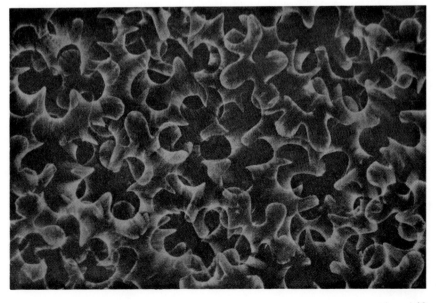

Illus. 65. Jig-saw shapes make an exciting design, which is heightened by the ice-cool blue pastel. The black construction paper gives an eerie feeling to the whole design.

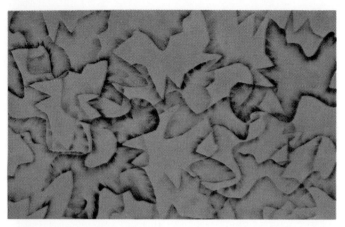

Illus. 66. The light blue provides a pleasing background for the dark blue pastel in this non-representational design.

In Illus. 66, almost the same light blue tone appears but here it is in the background paper, and the dark blue pastel merges into an excellent relationship of color. Black is only used for accent. Strong contrasts in value permit the observer to distinguish each shape from a distance.

An interesting approach in a stencilled design is obtained by applying both stencils A and B to the same location, causing the pastel color to radiate both *toward* and *away* from the center. (See Illus. 67.)

The stencilled shapes visible in Illus. 68 are especially interesting. Both stencils A and B were used to stencil the symmetrical design motifs, one jagged and one smooth and flowing.

Representational Designs

Illus. 69 reveals the stencil technique being used in two different ways. A single teardrop petal was cut from paper and then repeatedly placed around a focal point to form many blossoms. The edges of the blossoms created by stencil A were re-crayoned between each placement. Then the sheet from which the petals were cut, that is, stencil B, was used to form solid petals. Instead of rubbing inward from stencil B's edges in the

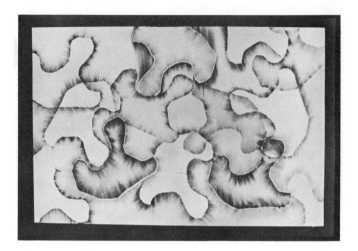

Illus. 67. The pastel colors radiate both toward and away from the center here.

usual manner, the crayon was stroked back and forth in the holes of stencil B to create shading. Dark stem lines, added to unify blossoms and leaves, were blurred by running a pencil eraser over them. Blurred lines com-

Illus. 68. Interesting symmetrical shapes were stencilled with an A and a B stencil onto yellow paper, using orange pastel colors.

Illus. 69. Paper stencils were used in two different ways to achieve the open and solid forms of the blossoms and leaves.

plement the blossom petals more effectively than a hard, rigid line would.

With young children of primary and intermediate grades, figures such as animals, trees and people are often conveyed by means of the crayon stencil technique.

Illus. 70. A crayoned worm rests upon a stencilled toadstool.

Illus. 71. Fluorescent crayons on black construction paper are especially striking in the stencil technique.

Use stiff paper, and let the students cut or tear recognizable shapes.

A little lazy worm rests upon a toadstool enjoying the view in Illus. 70. Coral-colored pastels were used to stencil the large flower blossoms. Shades of blue-green, green and dark green outline the grass and foliage.

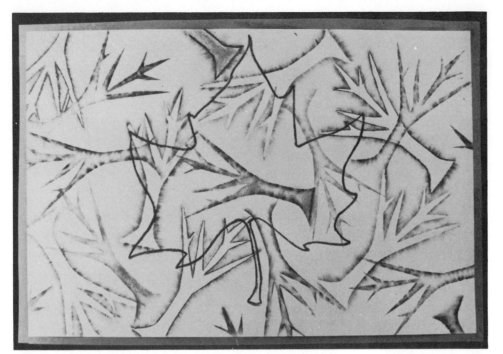

Illus. 72. **Dark green tree shapes in harmonious positions were stencilled on chartreuse paper, using stencils A and B. A superimposed outlined leaf provides a strong focal point in the middle of the composition, contributes a new and different form, and serves to tie together the various parts of the design.**

Fluorescent crayons have been used to stencil the basket of flowers on the black construction paper in Illus. 71. The orange, pink, green, yellow and green fluorescents appear most brilliant against the dark contrasting background. In Illus. 72 observe how interesting the shapes are and how related they appear.

Combining the Stencil Technique and Crayon Relief Technique

A textured area is fine to emphasize certain shapes outlined by the stencil technique; emphasis is an important design principle. In Illus. 73, crayon was stencilled on paper placed over a mesh vegetable bag. The side of the crayon was rubbed within certain stencilled shapes so as to duplicate the texture and pattern of the bag beneath.

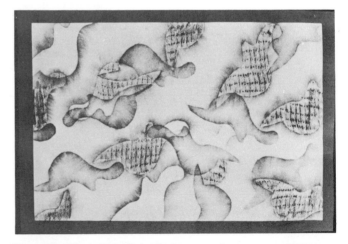

Illus. 73. The stencil technique and crayon relief were combined to create this design. A mesh vegetable bag was placed under the stencilled design to achieve the relief pattern in selected areas.

46

Illus. 74. On top of a collage (colored tissue paper shapes pasted onto a background), similar stencilled crayon forms were used to decorate the design.

Combining the Stencil and Collage Techniques

Collage had its birth in France. The French words "papiers collés" refer to papers and other materials that are pasted or glued to a background. The collage technique had its birth early in the 20th century when it was first explored by French cubists who pasted matchboxes, bus tickets, playing cards, etc., onto a background, creating an unusual composition to which they added dabs of color and related lines. The technique spread to Germany and later to the U.S.

The collage technique combines beautifully with the crayon stencil technique, as is evidenced in Illus. 74–78. The crayon stencil is used to define, emphasize and decorate the basic shapes cut out and pasted down as a collage.

In Illus. 74, black and light green starlike shapes were cut out of tissue paper and pasted on a background of white paper. Then three different paper stencils were cut in similar contours. Over the green tissue paper shapes, red wax crayon was stencilled; over the black tissue paper, white crayon was stencilled; and black crayon was stencilled over the white (blank) or negative spaces. In this composition, observe how the overlapping stencilled outlines unite all black, light green and white areas. While the stencilled shapes echo the basic paper shapes, they also provide a strong contrast in color, and create a diversity of shape and size not attainable with collage alone.

Butterfly shapes were torn from magenta and aqua-blue tissue paper for Illus. 75. A third hue, purple, was obtained by overlapping the two colors of tissue. A butterfly-shaped stencil was cut for the repeat outline which was established with black wax crayon.

A salt-water fish design is portrayed in Illus. 76. A single fish shape was used throughout the composition to illustrate how variety can be achieved even though only a single shape is used. Green and chartreuse paper fish shapes were first pasted onto white paper. Next, parts A and B of the stencil were used to apply blue crayon streaks. You will observe that some of the crayon streaks fan inward, towards the middle of the fish, whereas

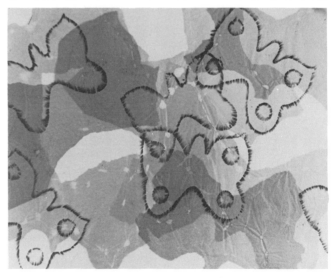

Illus. 75. Butterfly shapes torn from blue and magenta tissue paper were pasted down. Then a stencilled butterfly shape was crayoned over the torn shapes, uniting the various elements.

Illus. 76. Green and chartreuse paper fish shapes were pasted to the surface in this stencilled collage. An identical shape was rhythmically stencilled over the paper shapes and background.

placed and rubbed to achieve the many petals. A few petal shapes in the smaller sizes were outlined in black with India ink to provide a focal point. When the stencilling process was finished, the white background seemed too light in conjunction with the light-colored blossoms. Consequently, the artist used a brown crayon to solidly color many of the blank areas. The dark brown negative areas blend with the orange and yellow blossoms, and seem to draw the eye back into space, thereby creating the illusion of the third dimension, depth.

others radiate outwards. The stencilled shapes unite the green paper shapes with the white background and provide a rhythmic flow of line.

Daffodils provide the subject matter in Illus. 77. The delicate design was achieved with pale yellow tissue paper pasted onto white paper. A daffodil-shaped stencil was used to apply the red, wax-crayoned outlines. You will notice that no attempt was made to follow the yellow tissue paper shape with the stencil. This hit-and-miss application of stencilled outline over colored paper shapes creates a free, casual design. Other stencils, representing vertical grass and leaf foliage, were used to apply green and brown crayon in the bottom half of the composition. Delicate India-ink outlines of some of the stencilled edges afford a pleasing contrast against the bolder, stencilled, radiating lines.

An exceptionally interesting design was achieved by means of collage and crayon stencil techniques in Illus. 78. Yellow and orange daisy shapes were first pasted on white paper. For each size blossom, a single petal, cut from paper, provided the stencil. This was repeatedly

Illus. 77. Daffodils, torn from yellow tissue, brighten this design. Stencilled blossom shapes and foliage were added, and India ink used for a light decorative line.

Illus. 78. Yellow and orange flowers, cut from tissue, were pasted onto a white background. Then stencilled flower forms were crayoned over the surface and India ink drawings added. Most of the background, negative areas were colored a dark brown, and the border was co-ordinated.

Illus. 79. Leaves of varying sizes seem to be falling from the trees. The larger leaves are made of tissue paper, pasted on, and the smaller ones are stencilled on with crayon.

A yellow and brown border beautifully echoes the chosen colors within.

Illus. 79 was inspired by the autumn season. Multi-colored leaf shapes were cut from black and green sheets of tissue paper. Manila paper was used for the background. Using a smaller similarly-shaped stencil, white crayon was streaked onto the black and green colored leaves. Also included in the composition are pink leaves cut from tissue, adorned with green stencil images of a leaf pattern. Additional black and green stencilled leaf images overlap the collage leaves and the negative areas, tying both the leaves and the background together.

Just a few approaches have been presented here for using the stencil technique with crayon. Experimentation will lead to many other ideas in executing the stencil technique, which provides one of the most enjoyable avenues for the artist to explore with crayon.

CHAPTER FIVE

Exploring with the Mosaic Technique

A mosaic is a picture or design made by inlaying small bits of colored stone or glass, called tesserae, in mortar. Crayons may be used to simulate this ancient technique. In this chapter, we will make mosaics of crayoned tesserae where the crayon has been rubbed on paper, melted and painted on, poured on, or sliced.

First, plan your mosaic design. Using a light-colored crayon, draw a cartoon-like design on paper or such stiff materials as wallboard, plywood or cardboard. Create shapes which can be filled easily with small pieces of crayoned paper, or sliced crayon bits, the tesserae of the crayon mosaic. Keep the shapes as simple as possible because the outlines of the tesserae will make the composition quite busy and detailed.

In choosing colors, consider ways to achieve contrasts. Juxtapose cool blues and greens with warm reds, browns, oranges and yellows. Use light areas of color next to dark groupings of tesserae. Display contrasts in color values, so that all of the mosaic's shapes will show up vividly, even from a distance.

Contrast may also result from varying the sizes of the crayoned tesserae—some large, some minute. The total pattern takes on added interest when areas of small tesserae are juxtaposed with areas of large tesserae.

Preparing Rubbed-on Tesserae

Rub a solid color of crayon on one sheet of paper. Cover a second sheet with another crayon color, etc. For interesting variety, color some sheets lightly and other sheets heavily. When all your chosen colors have been rubbed on separate sheets of paper, cut the crayoned sheets into various-sized tesserae. You are now ready to paste the crayoned shapes onto your designed background.

The mosaic in Illus. 80, created from crayoned sheets

Illus. 80. Notice how, in this crayon-rubbed mosaic, the green tesserae are not only different in size but also in color, weight and value. So are the browns. All were cut from crayoned sheets and pasted onto a designed background of black paper.

of paper, represents an aerial view of a country scene. Fields, crops, a road, trees and a small red barn are represented by clusters of tesserae on black construction paper. Observe the placement of the various tesserae: some shapes run in a horizontal direction, others in a vertical direction, while some run diagonally.

The proud, lanky, stylish bird pictured in Illus. 82 was likewise created from tesserae cut from crayon-rubbed paper, but the total effect is quite different from Illus. 80. Observe all the tiny tesserae applied to the bird. His tail, back feathers, breast feathers, legs and head-tuft all display different tesserae patterns.

In Illus. 1 on page 4, a sailboat on the evening waters, a single color for the waters would have been monotonous. The artist has realized this and has, therefore, used many shades of blue and blue-green. These subtle color variations are likewise in the design's other areas. The sails are orange and yellow-orange, the boat is green and chartreuse. The moon and distant sailboat repeat and balance the dominant orange colors of the large sailboat. The sky is a mixture of blue, blue-grey and white tesserae, with the white representing flying sea gulls.

Mosaic designs become intensely alive when subtle

Illus. 81. Melted dark navy blue crayon was painted on paper to create the interesting shape of the carousel horse's body. Melted yellow was used for the horse's mane and tail. The plain background accentuates the positive shape of the horse.

Illus. 82. The crayon has been applied heavily to the various sheets of paper so that the tesserae are waxy and pronounced in their color. Much of the negative space has been left plain, causing the positive shapes—the bird, plants and mountains—to show vividly against the subdued background. Variety in the tesserae lends interest to the design.

51

color variations are contained in a single shape. This marks the difference between the work of a professional and a beginning artist. Try not to fill a shape with a single color. Instead, use a family of colors which are close in hue and value. For instance, use green with chartreuse, use light, dark, bright and dull shades of blue together, and let red, maroon and dark pink occupy another area.

Illus. 83. Melted colors were mixed to create the variegated tones suggesting the folds of Christ's robe. Redbrown and dark brown colors were painted and blended on paper to make the tesserae.

Illus. 84. Many interesting features are visible in the French poodle. A limited range of colors was effectively repeated and balanced. Throughout the composition, a variety of tesserae of different sizes and shapes were placed with artistic taste.

Illus. 85. This bird upon a treetop makes use of the wax-layer approach. Each wax piece is about one-eighth inch thick, and has been made by pouring molten wax onto a shell of tin foil. The broken bits are then glued to a sheet of light blue cardboard. The mosaic provides a texture which observers like to touch—they can feel the large, raised pieces of wax.

Tesserae of Melted Wax Crayon Painted on Paper

A second method for preparing your tesserae involves the use of melted crayon. Place peeled, broken, cast-off crayons in empty fruit juice cans of suitable size. Be certain that the colors are kept pure, that is, do not mix your colors. Place only yellow crayons in one fruit juice can, etc. Place the crayon-filled cans in a pan of water. Add water to a level just below the rims of the tin cans, or just high enough to prevent the cans from floating. Place the pan with the cans on the stove and allow the water to come to a boil. Heat until all of the crayons have melted within the separate cans. Remove the pan from the stove and place it on pads of newspaper on your worktable. The hot water will keep the crayons in a molten stage for quite some time.

Using a stiff bristle brush, paint the melted wax on sheets of drawing paper, one color per sheet. The wax will quickly harden. Then you can cut the paper into the desired shapes, and apply as tesserae onto your background design. The melted-wax approach allows you to use thick, waxy, vibrant colors. The final design may be rubbed with a cloth or paper towel, causing the wax to

shine and glow. But rub gently, so that the tesserae do not become crushed or separated from the background.

The melted-wax approach was used to create the figure of Christ, seen in Illus. 83. The heavily waxed paper tesserae were placed on a black sheet of construction paper, causing the bright colors to show up vividly against the plain negative areas.

Tesserae of Melted Crayon Layers

A third approach in the execution of a crayon mosaic involves the use of melted crayon without the paper backing. Heat your crayons in the same manner. Pour the melted wax onto a sheet of tin foil or tagboard, allowing the build-up of a layer $\frac{1}{8}$-inch thick or less. (Take caution during the pouring process, as the wax is extremely hot and can cause severe burns to the hands. Use a pot holder to grip the cans.) When the wax layer has hardened, bend the tin foil so that the layer breaks into small pieces of hard colored wax. The tin foil may be re-used. Then, with rubber cement or white liquid glue,

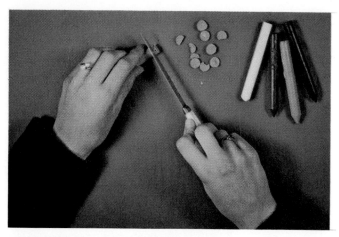

Illus. 86. Roll the crayon back and forth under a heated knife blade to create a groove around the crayon. Then, slice the crayon through on the groove.

Illus. 87. With white glue, the colorful crayon slices have been adhered to a wallboard backing.

paste the wax tesserae to a stiff background. (See Illus. 2 on page 4.)

The wax-layer method is not recommended for use in the elementary classroom. The handling and pouring of hot, molten wax is far too dangerous for young students, even when closely supervised. The painted paper approach might be tried by the later elementary student, however, since the hot wax remains in the tin cans and is applied with a brush. But again, a word of caution: a drop of molten wax upon the arm can be most painful.

Tesserae of Sliced Crayon

A fourth approach to mosaics is with chopped or sliced wax crayons, an excellent means of using up left-over crayons. Peel the crayons and chop them into small pieces with a knife. Heat your metal knife blade over a lighted candle to facilitate the cutting process. Press the heated knife on the peeled crayon and rock the crayon back and forth to establish a groove completely around the crayon. Then, press down until the crayon breaks on the slice where the groove is located. (See Illus. 86.)

Create pieces which are even in size, and make certain that the ends are flat and smooth. Apply glue to the end of each circular piece and arrange them into a colored mosaic. Plywood or heavy cardboard provides an effective backing.

Illus. 87 shows a finished mosaic created in this manner. The slices have been glued to a wallboard backing to create the star-like form. A border of yellow crayon slices ties in the edges, and the contrasting texture of white broken crayon pieces fills the background area.

Making a Mosaic Transfer Design

If your mosaic has been created by the tesserae of melted wax crayons on paper, it is fun next to create a transfer design from the finished product. Place a thin sheet of paper, such as newsprint, over the mosaic design. Run a warm iron over the newsprint, so that the wax will melt slightly. Each of the tesserae shapes of the original mosaic design will be clearly imprinted upon the second sheet of paper. There will be plenty of colored wax on the original tesserae which can easily be transferred to the print design. The other mosaic techniques do not always supply enough wax for a transfer design, and the tesserae may be separated from the backing.

It should be evident by now that the crayon is truly a remarkable tool for creating a mosaic. Experimentation will lead to other exciting discoveries as the crayon is used to explore the mosaic technique.

Illus. 89. In creating this transfer design, the artist observed that her white tesserae did not show up nearly so well when transferred. White wax against a blue background is quite vivid, but contrast was lost when the white wax was transferred to the white background. To remedy the problem, she used a ball point pen to outline some of the white shapes.

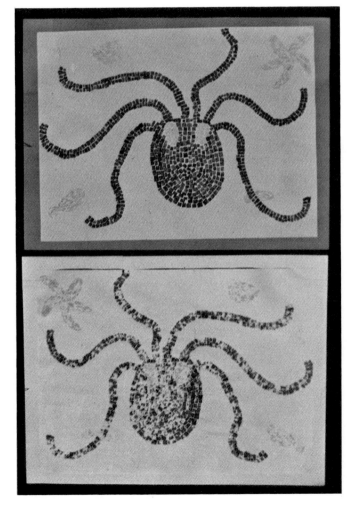

Illus. 88. This octopus was duplicated by means of the transfer technique. Melted wax was painted onto paper in creating the tesserae of the original design, seen at the top. With the application of heat, the crayoned mosaic design was transferred onto newsprint, thereby creating the second octopus, below.

CHAPTER SIX

Exploring with Background Materials

In further exploring with crayon, you will enjoy experimenting on a variety of background materials. This can do much to stimulate interest in texture and pattern. Each material has a "feel" of its own. Each material has its own shade and tint of color, which stimulates the artist to choose just the right complementary hues in crayon. Some materials also possess a pattern which can be blended beautifully with the added crayon design. Exciting things begin to happen when you carefully choose unique and interesting background materials for your crayon drawings.

Papers and Their Effect upon Crayon

Each type of paper has a unique surface character. This allows for diverse textural effects when crayon is applied. Newsprint is thin and somewhat smooth in texture. Thick, rich, smooth layers of wax can be applied

Illus. 90. Each type of paper has a unique surface character which affects the textural quality of applied crayon. Here, wax crayon was applied heavily to manila paper, and the design was shined by rubbing a paper towel over its surface. The total design is waxy, unpenetrable, opaque, rich and lustrous.

easily, but a rough, grainy texture is more difficult to obtain. Manila paper and white drawing paper have a toothy surface, allowing you to achieve a variety of textural effects within a single composition. Corrugated cardboard has a ribbed pattern, which may become further pronounced when crayon is applied.

Search for as many different kinds of paper as you can find. Experiment with crayon on the surfaces to see which paper contributes most to the effect you are aiming for.

The value and textural character of a crayon color may be determined by the amount of pressure you apply in drawing. Delicate, timid areas of color may contrast with areas that are nearly impasto. In looking again at Illus. 31 on page 24, you will notice that crayon has been lightly applied to manila paper to achieve a light transparent effect. In Illus. 29 on page 23, crayon was both heavily and lightly applied to achieve opaque and transparent effects on manila paper. Illus. 90 shows crayon very heavily applied with pressure over the entire surface of manila paper. But something else was also done which you will want to try. A paper towel was crushed and then rubbed vigorously over the heavy-crayoned surface, causing the wax to shine. Polishing the drawing with toweling or cloth gives it a smooth, shiny, jewel-like surface. Colors become unusually brilliant, intense and sparkling. They resemble high-gloss enamels or oil paints.

Oiled Paper (Window Transparencies)

Select a thin sheet of white drawing paper and draw a colorful crayon design upon its surface. Using a brush, paint a thin layer of cooking oil upon the paper either before or after the drawing process. The oil will cause the paper to appear more transparent, thereby admitting more light when the oiled design is placed against a windowpane. Sunlight, shining through the oiled paper, causes the crayon design to come alive in its boldness.

Illus. 91. Beautiful transparencies can be created when crayon is applied to oiled paper. Placed over a window, the wax crayon designs stand out boldly against the transparent background.

Illus. 92. Cloths such as canvas, linen and cotton, provide excellent backgrounds. This design was heavily applied to cotton. The peeled side of the crayon was used for the background color.

Cloth

You will find that color is most effectively applied to cloth when the crayon stroke follows the weave of the cloth. Glue or tack canvas, linen, tarlatan or cotton to thick paper or cardboard before crayoning.

The colors may be set by placing the fabric face down on clean paper, and using a hot iron on the reverse side. The iron may be lifted as each section is pressed. Bits of colored cloth, yarn and string may be sewed or glued onto the crayon drawing to accent the design.

Interesting effects can be obtained by dyeing the crayon design in cold water dye. The wax of the crayon will resist the dye and the design will shine brilliantly through a background which has been dyed.

A really different cloth is surgical crinoline, which has a textured surface like canvas, but is much lighter, more supple and much less expensive. It takes the wax of the crayon in a most inviting way. If you use crinoline (which comes in rolls 1 yard wide) unmounted, stroke with the crayon in a single direction. Better, attach the crinoline to tagboard or construction paper with liquid starch. When dry, the soft threads remain in place as you rub the crayon back and forth. The light paper backing, moreover, allows the crayon design to be seen more readily.

Crushed Paper Bags

The texture and color of paper bags unite beautifully with linear, geometric designs rendered with wax

Illus. 93. Line designs with void areas such as this might adorn a shirt or blouse. A hot iron will set the colors.

Illus. 94. A delicate, repeat design applied with crayon. The threads of the cotton cloth are visible since the design is lightly applied. The crayon strokes strongly suggest the many delicate threads of a tapestry, an illusion of needlework.

Illus. 95. Parallel vertical and horizontal creases will help in laying out a geometric design on a crushed, dried paper bag.

crayons. Soak the bag first in warm water to loosen the glue, enabling you to separate the seams and make one long sheet of unfolded paper. Then crush the water-soaked, unfolded brown bag in your hands. Open the bag and crumple it once again in your fist. Repeat the crushing process several times. Finally, open up the bag, smooth it out and place it on newspaper to dry.

Illus. 95 shows how to lay out a design. Crayon on the bag as you would on any rough surface. Finished crayon designs on paper bags make excellent book covers. They are also strongly reminiscent of Polynesian cloth, or tapa, as it is called.

Illus. 96, a finished design, illustrates how beautifully the chosen colors complement the natural tan color of the bag. You can see how the vertical and horizontal creases have aided the artist in planning his geometric repeat design. Note that the paper bag retains many of the creases introduced during the crumpling process.

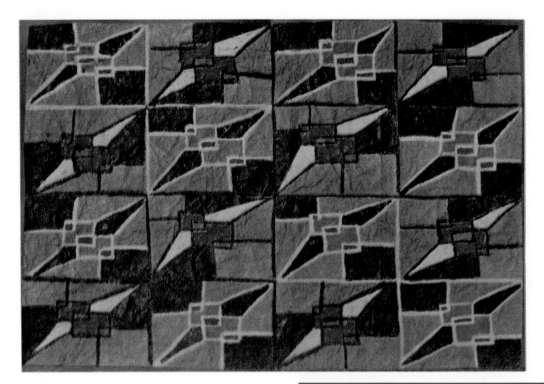

Illus. 96. It looks like leather, but it's just a crushed paper bag. Colors such as red, orange, white, purple, green and browns appear especially beautiful on this background. Geometric designs fit neatly between parallel folds.

Illus. 97. A crayoned paper bag with a rhythmic pattern. Plain solid colors fill triangular and moon-shaped areas to create a strong diagonal movement.

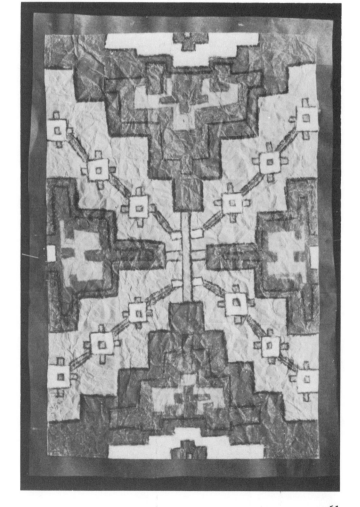

Illus. 98. Every attempt was made to cover completely the natural color of the paper bag. Pink, blue and red adorn the many rectangles created by folding the paper. This is a rather large work, measuring 2 feet by 2 feet.

Illus. 99. Indian art has had an influence upon the artist here. The geometric designs strongly suggest the pottery, tepee and blanket designs executed by some American Indians.

These creases cause the material to look like leather. Observe, too, how the natural tan color of the paper bag can become an integral part of the design, as in Illus. 96.

The design pictured in Illus. 3 on page 5 is unique in that line is the only element used to adorn the surface. Diagonal, vertical and horizontal lines divide the area into a series of rectangles which are dominated and united by dark brown diagonal lines running from top to bottom. See how the white, green, yellow, red and brown colors are juxtaposed.

Oblongs, zig-zags and variations on the diamond shape fit into the parallel fold designs too. The color scheme can be very limited, but variety in tone can be achieved by introducing heavy black lines with lightly applied grey areas. Some shapes can be revealed by a blend of strong color like orange, covered with light black. The paper bag can often provide a border which relates beautifully with the crayoned design.

Illus. 100. Variations on the diamond shape are evident in this design, which is crayoned with just black and orange. The natural tan of the paper bag shows through the design and the border is simply the tan crumpled paper.

Illus. 101. Indian signs and symbols—two tepees, two Indians and the sun—are visible among the geometric shapes. The basic triangle is grouped in a variety of ways.

Illus. 102. Spider-like creatures adorn every other rectangle. Black and orange legs radiate from a black body, and long, continuous diagonal lines tie all of the shapes together.

Illus. 103. A very large work, measuring close to 3 feet square. The total design is unusually interesting in that the artist has found endless ways to repeat a basic idea with a basic pattern. Certain shapes are repeated, but they are never repeated in exactly the same way. The colors, while rather limited in range, are tastefully repeated and balanced throughout the composition.

Paper Bag Puppets and Masks

Having seen how successfully crayon can be applied to crushed paper bags to create a 2-dimensional design, it would now be fun to create a 3-dimensional object from a crayoned dry paper bag. Leave the seams of the bag intact, but fold up the bottom of the bag to crayon facial features on. As in Illus. 104, draw the eyes and the upper lip on this surface.

Illus. 104 shows the bottom lip in closed position, and Illus. 105 with the puppet's mouth open. The ears or horns are created from the back side of the bag, which is slit and cut to shape after being crayoned. Black crayon is boldly used to outline the facial features, ears, beard and shirt pattern on the front side of the bag. Red crayon decorates the shirt, mouth and ears. By running your hand and fingers into the upturned bag, the bottom can be

manipulated in such a way as to synchronize mouth movements with the spoken word. (See Illus. 105.)

For a mask, choose a brown paper bag slightly larger than the intended wearer's head. Slip it over his or her head. Using crayon, mark the location of the eyes and mouth. Remove the bag now and proceed to cut away the eyes and mouth shape or color them in. Color the front and sides of the bag with a colorful geometric crayon design.

A lion's head decorates the paper bag mask seen in Illus. 106. Two cones cut from construction paper are taped to the top of the mask to suggest horns. Two symmetrical ears, cut from paper, are fastened to either side of the mask with brass paper fasteners. Narrow paper strips radiate from the nose as whiskers and echo the dark crayon lines which outline the color areas.

Illus. 104 (left). The bag puppet with its mouth closed, that is, with bag bottom facing forward.

Illus. 105 (right). With inserted fingers, you lift the bag's bottom from inside and the lips spread apart so the puppet can "talk."

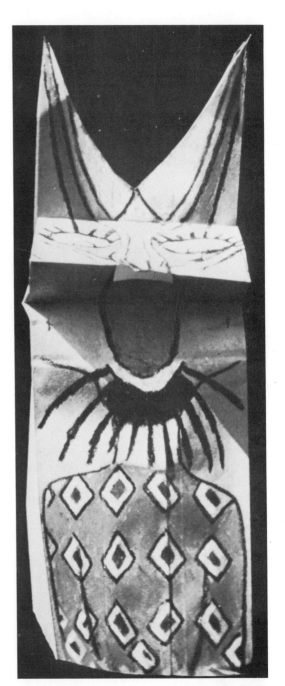

Paper Plates

For a change of pace, apply crayon to a circular paper plate. These lend themselves to arrangements making use of colorful borders surrounding a central motif. Lines usually radiate from a central figure; shapes, circles and dots might also fan out the same way. Crayon-decorated paper plates can be made to resemble a ceramic design. They may be used to adorn an end table, the television set or hi-fi, or hang on the wall of the kitchen or re-creation room.

When purchasing paper plates for crayoning, select those that do not have a waxy surface. Wax crayon will adhere better to a rough textured surface.

Illus. 107(a) and (b) show two colorful crayon designs executed on paper plates. In (a) yellow, orange and white shapes were colored upon the plate, using oil crayons. Next, a brush dipped in water was used to dissolve a brown colored water crayon, which was then painted completely over the crayoned design. The oil crayon colors resisted the brown wash, allowing the wash to remain only on the uncolored areas of the paper plate. Observe the interesting little bubbles of paint remaining on the colored shapes. In (b), red and green wax crayons were held over a burning candle and then quickly applied to the plate while still in a moulten state. A thickness of wax can best be obtained this way. Observe how the artist capitalized on the embossed, ribbed edge of the plate to cause white lines to radiate outward. The

Illus. 106. An exciting, geometric crayon design applied to a paper bag mask.

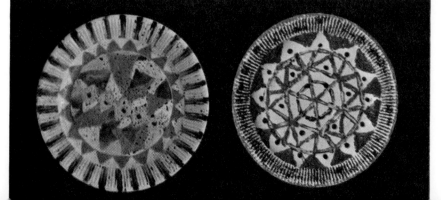

Illus. 107 (a) and (b). Oil crayon and water crayon were applied to the left paper plate (a). Melted wax crayon was used on the right-hand plate (b).

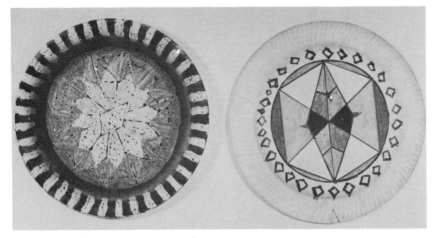

Illus. 108 (a) and (b). In (a) pink, purple and red oil crayons were used in combination with a black water crayon. The black was painted over the oil colors and covers only the un-crayoned portions of the plate. In (b), oil crayons were used to create the fine, controlled line design and the solid shapes of color.

wax was lightly applied only to the raised lines of the embossed border.

The Want Ads

Crayons and the want ad sections of the daily newspaper provide a fascinating combination of materials for exploring with design. The vertical lines separating the columns and the horizontal lines of fine print serve as guides in laying out the geometric shapes dictated by the artist's imagination. When the finished design is viewed from a short distance away the small print fuses and fades unobtrusively into the background, leaving a bold, colorful design of great aesthetic interest.

Illus. 109. Created by an elementary-grade student, this design is formal in balance. Children like to repeat shapes, colors and patterns on each side of the composition in an identical manner. This example reveals an interesting variation on the X motif. Four X-shapes are separated by a cross formation, with many small and large solid shapes adorning the structure.

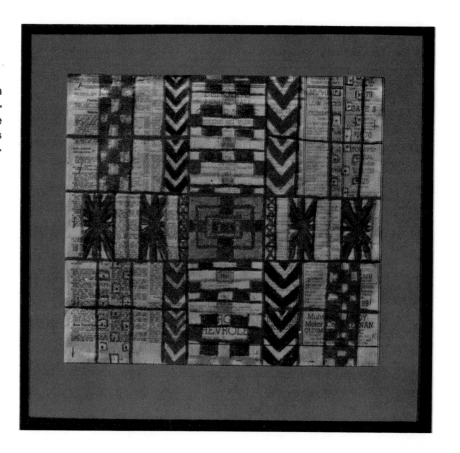

Illus. 110. The design appears to be formal in this student's work, but a careful study indicates that it has subtle differences on the left- and right-hand sides. These differences in the placement of the art elements contribute to the design's appeal.

Graph Paper and Crayon Pencil

Crayon pencils on graph paper allow you to create truly beautiful designs with vibrant, pulsating rhythms within geometric forms. Many of the designs suggest the craft articles which originate in the Scandinavian countries. Both children and adults enjoy the working process involved and the final effects. Some of the examples shown here were created by fifth-grade students.

The best graph paper for crayon pencil work is composed of horizontal and vertical light blue lines, evenly spaced ¼-inch apart. Plan your design for either horizontal or vertical rows of squares to be filled in with a single color or alternating light and dark colors. Try checkerboard patterns or diagonal rows of squares, or

dot, criss-cross, circle or diamond shapes within single squares. By uniting a number of the small squares, you can create larger square, triangular, circular and diamond shapes. Use thin pencil lines to cover the thin blue lines of the graph paper and to provide accent and variety.

The colors become extra rich and vibrant when the crayon pencil point is dipped into water just prior to filling in the square forms. Also, the colors flow more easily and are applied more quickly when the pencil crayon is moistened. A few of the crayon colors will remain light, chalky and dull even though water is used.

It is easy to construct a design which has a formal balance. With few exceptions, children's designs become formally balanced. By counting the blue lines or squares,

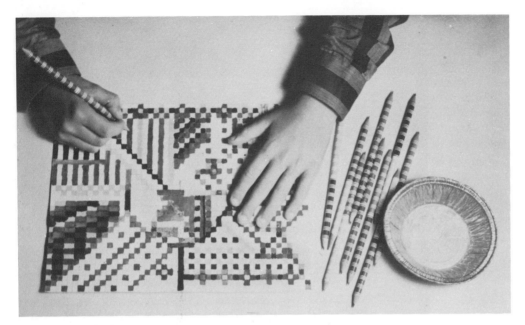

Illus. 111. Tim, grade five at the Wyoming, Mich., Parkview School, dips crayon pencils in water and then applies them to graph paper. Filling in the squares to create an interesting design is made easier by the grid pattern.

Illus. 112. Here small dots were placed in the middle of carefully chosen squares to emphasize certain areas and provide interesting variety.

Illus. 113. Although children usually like to create designs of formal balance, this informally balanced design with squares and dots is beautifully executed.

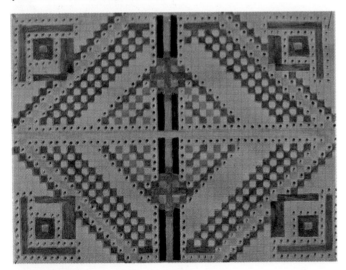

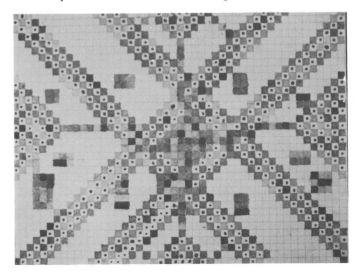

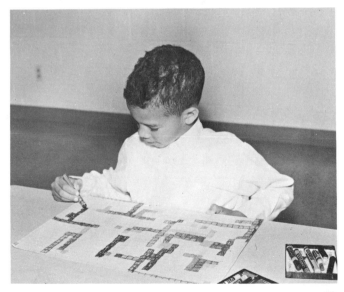

the children are easily able to locate the middle of the composition. This is the beginning point in some instances. Some students prefer to begin their design at the left side. They count a certain number of spaces from the left and top or bottom of the paper. The corresponding squares are easily located on the opposite side by counting. Other matching locations follow.

You need not feel that all spaces of the grid should be filled in. White areas and a plain background can be important parts of the design, for they offer the eye a rest from the lively color areas, and accent the busy areas by contrast.

You might be wise to choose just a few different colors in executing a design. This encourages the frequent repetition of colors, providing unity, balance and continuity of design.

Graph Paper and Wax Crayon

Graph paper is available in various sizes. So far, we have seen only ¼-inch squares used, but graph paper containing larger (½-inch or 1-inch) squares may best suit the creative needs of the younger primary-grade student. And instead of using pencil crayons, the younger pupil might like to use wax crayons. Illus. 117 was created by a third-grade student on ½-inch squares.

The classroom teacher might rule his own graph paper by drawing horizontal and vertical lines on a master copy and running off the grids on a copying machine. The teacher can choose a suitable paper and over-all size.

Illus. 115B. This design strongly suggests the beautiful woven patterns rendered by Scandinavians in their sweaters and other apparel.

Illus. 116. A number of the squares have been covered with strong, bold, blue triangular forms. Being large in size, these forms accent the design and provide a pleasing variety within the composition.

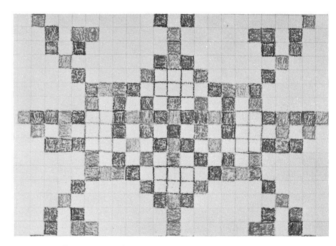

Illus. 117. Children of the primary grades enjoy using wax crayon on large-square graph paper. Their attention spans are short and coordination between hand and eye is not yet fully developed. Consequently, grid paper having large squares best suits their needs.

Graph Paper and Numerical Designs

Repeated numbers, when adorned with crayoned shapes and lines, may be beautifully transformed into rhythmic designs. The project may even be turned into a profitable arithmetic lesson. In Illus. 119, for example, the fact that 2 plus 3 equals 5 was used. Observe how the equation was repeated in the 1-inch squares of the grid paper. Certain parts of the numbers were filled in with solid colors while other parts were left plain, so that an interesting rhythmic design emerges.

Illus. 120 is an attempt to cover the grid paper completely with crayon, allowing little of the background to peer through. Nine plus 7 equals 16 is the theme. Solid areas and open line areas combine to provide an exciting contrast, which is accentuated by the artist's choice of colors.

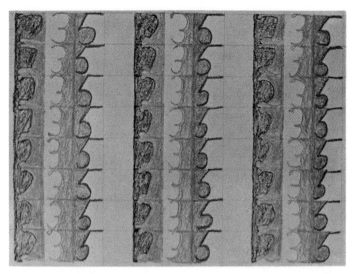

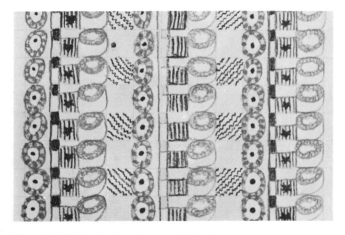

Illus. 118. This design is especially interesting because of the variety of patterns which decorate the various numbers.

Illus. 119. When the numbers are filled in with crayon color, their shape blends into the design. For instance, the outline of the 2 is here hardly discernible.

Illus. 120 (below). Nine plus 7 equals 16 in this beautifully embellished and colorful design. The vertical lines tend to "lose" the numbers.

"Six plus 4 equals 10" is the theme portrayed in the repeat design of Illus. 118. And what an interesting design it is! Small circles fill the circular portion of the 6. A star and stripes, suggesting the flag, adorn the square portion of some number 4's. A solid shape fills the lower portion of the upright figure of 4 which also serves as the one in the figure 10. An alternating light and dark, minute circle design embellishes the zero (in 10). And each vertical column of equations is connected by alternating

Illus. 121. Sandpaper gives a natural rough texture to crayon art. Here checks and stripes provide a busy background.

blocks of wavy, diagonal lines. All of the varying elements help to capture the attention of the viewer.

The graph paper contributes to easy construction of an exciting number design. The process always leads to pleasant surprises. When beginning, the artist has little conception of the final results. Try it!

Sandpaper

Sandpaper provides one of the most exciting surfaces you can use in applying crayon. Sandpapers come in a variety of grains and colors, ranging from coarse to fine, and black to tan. The lighter colors are preferable for crayon. As for textures, each affects the application of crayon in a different manner: coarse sandpapers are best for rough, textural patterns, whereas fine sandpapers allow for a more subtle, detailed application of the wax. Varying the pressure on the crayon further enables you to create variety in texture and pattern.

Heavy, dense, shiny areas of wax crayon may be juxtaposed with light, open, pale areas of color as in Illus. 123. The natural tan color of the sandpaper would shine through were the background not completely covered with a light cover of yellow. When crayon is lightly applied to a fine-grain sandpaper, it creates a transparent film of color.

In Illus. 121, a four-petalled flower design is the focal point. The negative and positive background areas form a pattern of alternating darks and lights, so that the broad solid areas of the petals contrast beautifully with the busy, detailed background.

Illus. 122 is much plainer in concept. Its broad, solid areas of color fill geometric shapes in a light, transparent manner.

Illus. 122. In this simple geometric design with broad areas of color, white crayon covers the otherwise blank areas of the sandpaper.

Sandpaper Transfer Designs

Wax-crayon-on-sandpaper designs are ideal for experimenting with transfer prints. Lay a sheet of plain newsprint paper down on a hard flat surface and place the original wax-on-sandpaper design on it. Apply a hot iron to the back of the sandpaper so that a little of the wax is transferred onto the newsprint. Pull the sheets apart. (See Illus. 126.) What a surprise to find that you now have two designs! The original has lost none of its beauty and the print reveals a new emphasis.

Experiment with the transfer technique using different sandpapers. (You can also place the sandpaper down and apply the iron to the newsprint.) Extremely coarse sandpapers will deposit a dotted pattern of color on the newsprint, while fine sandpapers will produce smoother tones. Vary the amount of heat by adjusting the dial on the iron. A hot iron, pressed down a number of seconds, will cause the wax to flow into all recesses of the sandpaper, producing a flowing, smooth design. A cooler iron, quickly applied, establishes a more textural design. Experiment! Invent! Create! Crayons and sandpaper provide many avenues for exploration in art.

Illus. 123. The yellow is applied lightly here, the brown more heavily, and the blues and red arrows heavy and dense to create a shine on the fine-grained sandpaper.

Illus. 124 (left). Both positive and negative shapes of this clown design on sandpaper are given careful consideration. Note the interesting free-form shapes in the background.

Illus. 125 (right). This design of various-sized overlapped legs is lightly applied on fine-grained sandpaper.

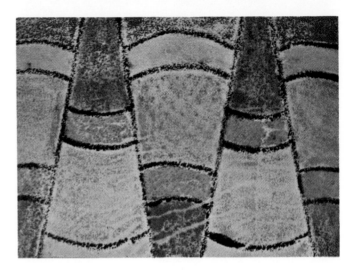

Illus. 127. This is the transferred print in somewhat muted colors and looking rougher in texture than the original because the iron was only lightly applied. Note that in the lower central portion of the picture, where the hot iron rested longer, the wax tended to melt and spread out.

Illus. 128. This is the original art on fine sandpaper.

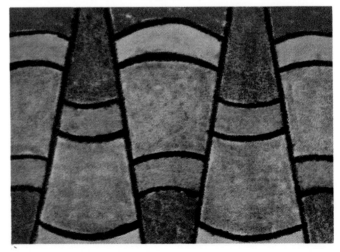

Illus. 126. The fun begins when a transfer print is made from the wax-crayoned sandpaper design. The original is placed face down on a clean sheet of absorbent paper such as newsprint. Rubbing the hot flatiron smoothly over the back of the original causes the sandpaper design to transfer its wax colors onto the new sheet of paper.

74

Illus. 129. From this bold, coarse sandpaper original, the transfer design in Illus. 130 was made.

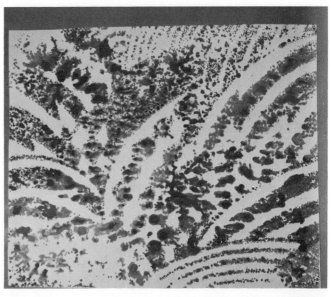

Illus. 130. This print has an extremely rough appearance (almost like Pointillism) because heat from the iron was applied only briefly, and many details were lost.

The brightly colored fruit design in Illus. 131 with pineapple, grapes, apples, pears and other fruits was difficult to transfer. The monoprint turned out to be especially beautiful, but it was so delicate with its rough pattern of wax that a black crayon had to be used to outline and emphasize the vague shapes of color. (Illus. 132.)

The interesting butterfly design depicted in Illus. 135 made the transfer to newsprint exceptionally well. Very little wax was lost in the transfer (Illus. 136) because the hot iron, heavily applied, caused the wax to be transferred in a smooth, non-textural manner.

Illus. 131 and 132. The sandpaper still life (left) came out so vague in the transfer process that it was necessary to define the shapes (right) with black crayon outlines.

75

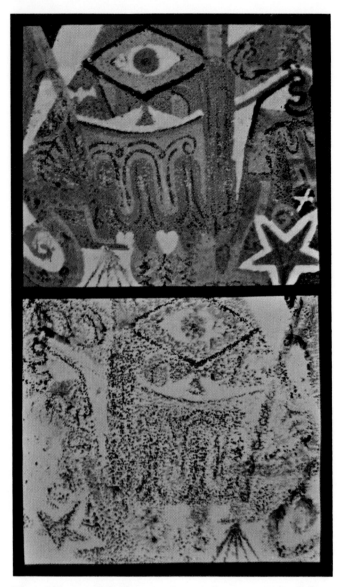

Illus. 133 and 134. How to "create" an ancient artifact. The Egyptian motif (top) in its original rich colors was an eye-catcher. When the iron was lightly applied, a delicate transfer print was obtained (below) which resembles a weathered mural or cave painting.

The design and its transfer pictured in Illus. 137 and 138 are especially interesting because a number of small scenes drawn upon black sandpaper have been juxtaposed on white paper. The white crayon appears most attractive upon the dark background. Black crayon was applied to the black sandpaper so that a black background would also appear in the transferred design.

In many prints, the colors will not be realistic, but the color effect will be dramatic. The print displays much less color intensity than the original. Its tone is likely to be more delicate and lighter in appearance.

Collage with Crayon and Sandpaper

Interesting results can be obtained by combining crayon and cut-out sandpaper shapes into a collage. The sandpaper is glued to a base paper—manila, newsprint or construction paper—either before or after being

Illus. 135 and 136. A lengthy application of heat to a butterfly design on fine sandpaper produced a distinct transfer print on newsprint.

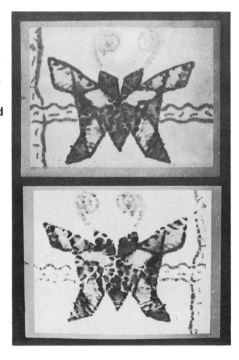

Illus. 137. A grouping of four separate but similar designs on black sandpaper.

Illus. 138. In transferring to white paper the designs are united into an interesting composition, with a totally different effect.

colored with crayon. Attractive color combinations and a 3-dimensional feel can be the result.

In Illus. 139 a more or less monochrome effect was achieved with this technique.

Throughout this chapter we have demonstrated in many ways that the choice of background materials can contribute immeasurably to the beauty of an applied crayon design. Try using the materials suggested here and search for new and unique materials. Discover which background materials work best for you.

Illus. 139. This is not a transfer design but a collage. The two fish shapes were cut from sandpaper and glued to a white paper background before being rubbed with orange crayon. The negative (white) areas in the background were crayoned with the peeled sides and ends of the same color crayon.

Illus. 140. Patti carefully cuts out a lion's form from tagboard to be used with the crayon relief technique to create a repeat pattern.

CHAPTER SEVEN

Exploring with Crayon Reliefs

Have you ever rubbed a pencil point over a thin sheet of paper with a penny beneath, so that the face on the coin distinctly appears on the paper? The crayon relief technique is executed in essentially the same manner. Simply substitute crayons and textured materials for the pencil and penny, and many new avenues for creating pattern and texture will be opened up. In making rubbed crayon drawings by the crayon relief technique a greater sensitivity to texture, pattern and the beauty of repeated design will be instilled in the artist.

Using Paper and Cardboard Shapes

Very young pupils of the primary grades find the crayon relief technique to their liking. Objects from their limited environment, such as pets, people, trees, holiday symbols, etc. may easily be cut from manila or construction paper and placed under a thin sheet of newsprint. By rubbing the broad side of a peeled crayon over the underlying form an impression of the paper's shape is picked up. One or two shapes may be repeated within a single composition, introducing the young child to the beauty of a repeated design. Experimentation will reveal that the broad side of a *short* crayon creates a more effective impression than that of a long one. Also, students sometimes find that a shape cut from a simple sheet of manila or construction paper leaves too indistinct an impression. Students should be encouraged to cut their shapes from three or four sheets of paper at one time to get adequate thickness for the object's edges to be sharply discerned as the crayon is rubbed.

Illus. 141 (right). With the tagboard shape placed beneath a sheet of newsprint, Patti uses a short, peeled red crayon, to rub her newsprint sheet so that the cardboard image appears on the paper.

Illus. 142 (below). The finished work reveals that each lion has been carefully placed to create a closely-knit, unified design.

Older children and adults will enjoy cutting their objects and shapes from cardboard, tagboard or poster-board. In Illus. 140–142, Patti shows how she creates a repeat pattern of an animal form which she cuts from tagboard. Each time she finishes rubbing the side of her crayon on the paper over the cardboard shape, she lifts the newsprint and repositions it to create the next image. She does not move the cardboard lion. Observe how Patti has carefully placed the lions so that they almost touch, thereby creating a united composition.

In Illus. 143 also note the fine unity of parts achieved by the close approximation of the giraffe shapes.

A roughly circular cardboard shape with the middle removed was used for Illus. 144. The cardboard was

Illus. 143. Tall, lanky giraffes come leaping through in this crayon relief.

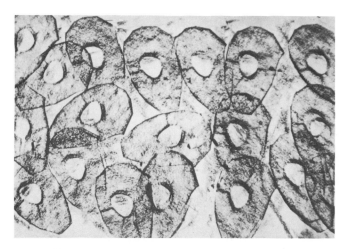

Illus. 144. A haphazard overlapping placement engenders a freer crayon relief design.

Illus. 145. Two crayons, red and dark green, were used to execute this relief design.

Illus. 146. This little insect is complete with crawling legs, protruding antennae and a curled tail for a humorous design.

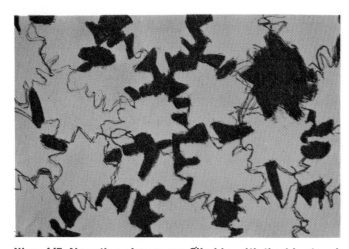

Illus. 147. Negative shapes are filled in with the blunt end of the red crayon to create variety.

placed in a haphazard manner so that the repeated shapes do not always touch along the edges of the adjacent shape. In some instances, they overlap and create new, small accidental forms which add a pleasant note of variety to the design.

Multi-colored designs are fun to create with the crayon relief technique. Illus. 145 pictures an interesting pattern with many irregular protrusions and positions. With two colors, too, interesting checkerboard patterns might be achieved. Alternate between the light and dark crayons when you move the cardboard shape.

When creating animal, human or insect forms, try exaggerating their features so as to create a comical effect, as in Illus. 146.

In creating Illus. 147, the artist used the *end* and point, but not the side of the crayon. In this design, some of the negative shapes (the spaces between the positive lines) were filled in with solid shapes of color to add contrast to the otherwise linear design.

The positioning of the octopus in Illus. 148 is unique. All the heads of the octopus radiate from the middle line of the paper along the top and bottom borders.

Unusual effects may come from folding your paper or cardboard prior to cutting, as in Illus. 150. A small piece of tagboard was folded twice to create the relief design, then notches were cut in the edges. The square shape was positioned so that a plain, uncolored margin appears between all the shapes.

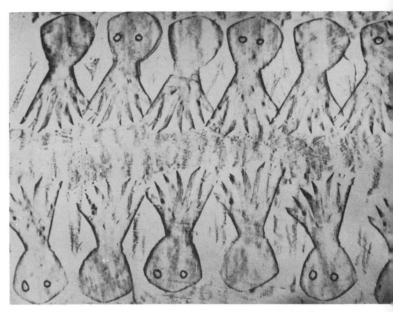

Illus. 148. Besides being arranged so that the octopus head touches the top and bottom borders, this composition is given emphasis by having circular, piercing eyes added to only some of the forms.

Illus. 150 (below). A folded tagboard sheet, with shapes cut away, was opened to provide the pattern for this handsome composition. Avenues are left between the patterns. The opened-out square is shown below the art.

Illus. 149. After a fish-shaped piece of cardboard was haphazardly moved under the newsprint, and the side of peeled blue and orange crayons rubbed over the surface, the result appeared rather timid. So black crayon outlining the contours of each shape was used to achieve a bolder effect and unify all parts of the design.

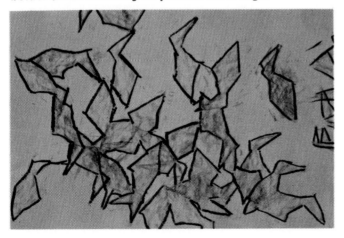

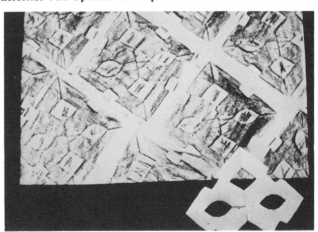

Using Textured Materials

Search your basement, attic, kitchen and school for materials that can produce exciting textures for crayon reliefs, and store them when you find them in a box labelled "Textures." Mesh from orange and potato bags, netting, burlap, vegetable graters, fly swatters, pieces of screen, bamboo window shades, place mats—all produce vivid textures. Experimentation will prove which materials are most effective for your next project.

Students might take a "looking walk" around the school. What textures might the hall walls provide? Is the sidewalk an interesting texture? The floor mats near

the door? The frosted window in the bathroom? Wherever you look, you will notice textures of diverse character. The grillwork of the radiator cover, the surfaces of a brick wall, the small tiles of the bathroom floor, the cover of an encyclopedia volume, a sewer lid—all

Illus. 152. In this winter scene by Mike, a fifth-grade student, a mesh orange sack under paper was rubbed to create the tree and home patterns. A heater grill provided the pattern for the roadway. The sky was cut away so that the blue construction paper background could become visible.

Illus. 153. To suggest fish within a net, various-sized fish shapes were cut from cardboard and placed over a mesh vegetable bag. The bag was first cut open to form a large flat surface. With newsprint placed over all, the artist merely rubbed with the side of a black crayon.

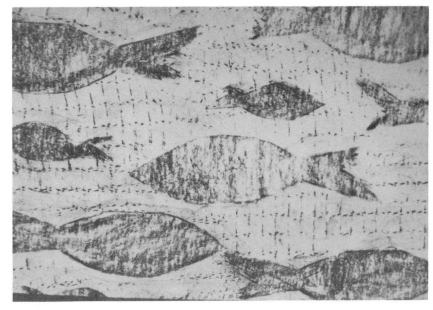

Illus. 154 (below). The background sheet of this collage is completely covered with juxtaposed shapes of textured newsprint. A plastic doily, grill of a furnace filter, the back of a wicker chair, the grill work of a radiator, an ash tray, the mesh of a potato bag, and netting were used to create the various overlapping patterns, which were cut out and pasted on.

display a texture unique unto the material itself. Experiences with the crayon relief technique train the artist to really see what is around him. Design consciousness develops as the textured impressions are assembled in an aesthetic, pleasing manner.

Using Cardboard and Textured Materials Together

Exciting things begin to happen when cardboard silhouettes are placed over textured materials such as mesh bags or screening. The crayon not only picks up the impressions of the cardboard objects, but it reveals the textured background as well. Solid, accenting shapes are combined with a delicate, contrasting textural background. Illus. 153 illustrates what exciting effects may be achieved this way.

Creating a Crayon Relief Collage

We have seen how shapes and textures may be created by the relief technique on a single sheet of paper. In exploring the technique further, we find that the same technique can be used effectively to create collages. You can cut various shapes from crayon-textured and -colored papers and join them into a single composition.

Illus. 155. A collage may be assembled by pasting together cut shapes from different sheets of newsprint on which you have created unlike patterns by means of the crayon relief technique.

imprint on the shoe shapes. A waffle iron grill was used in creating the shirt. Part of a plastic doily provided the hat with its pattern. All were assembled and were pasted on a background of light blue construction paper.

Materials from nature can be combined with textured materials to create crayon relief collages. In Illus. 156, the leaves of a tree were plucked green so as to capture the subtle vein patterns. After the leaf textures were crayon rubbed on paper, another piece of newsprint was placed over a mesh vegetable bag, a handkerchief design, a rough brick wall and a piece of string. From the various sheets of newsprint, hat shapes were cut out (using the real leaf outlines as a pattern) and juxtaposed and overlapped upon a surface of construction paper to form a single collage.

Two romantic figures ice skate beneath the beams of a shining moon in Illus. 157, as a third figure approaches the scene. A row of yellow lights surrounds the ice and

Illus. 156. The actual leaves of a tree were used to create the basic shapes and vein patterns of this crayon relief work. The other patterns were added later.

In creating a person, the skirt or trousers may be cut from one sheet of paper, the shirt or blouse, hair, etc., from other textured papers. To create a non-representational composition, an older child or adult may repeat, join, and balance various interesting shapes cut from different textured papers.

In Illus. 155, a coarse piece of cloth provided the crayon pattern for the trousers. A mesh vegetable bag left its

Illus. 157 (above). A fifth-grader crayoned these three skaters, with patterns created in relief from a plastic doily, and then pasted up the collage.

Illus. 158 (left). Diverse textured surfaces contribute to the beautiful patterns in this underwater collage. The artist has used wavy lines to suggest water movement.

Illus. 159 (below). Op Art in the relief technique, with a furnace filter and a mesh vegetable bag as the basic materials.

serves to illuminate the skating stars. The fifth-grade artist has used different plastic doilies to create the patterns for her figures' garments.

A plastic doily, mesh vegetable bag, cut-glass bowl and waffle iron grill were used to create the beautiful fish, ocean plants and sea shells pictured in Illus. 158. The black construction paper background causes the bright crayon colors and patterns to stand out in a vivid, exciting, bold manner.

Creating Op Art

Within the last few years, Op Art has appeared in large art galleries and in leading magazines. This art form is

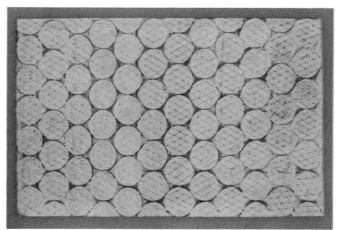

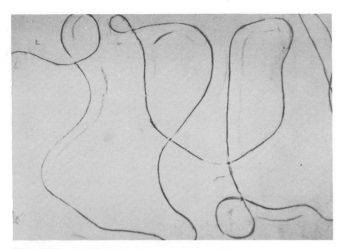

Illus. 160. A string has been arranged beneath newsprint, and the peeled side of a black wax crayon has been used to duplicate the raised line design on the paper.

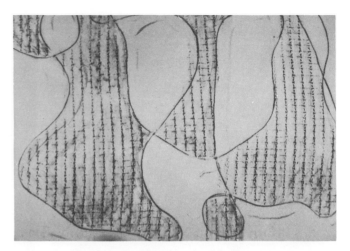

Illus. 161. The paper with the line design from Illus. 160 has been carefully placed over a mesh vegetable bag so that chosen areas defined by the line might be filled with pattern.

not easy to view because strong contrasts of color (often black and white too) are juxtaposed in such a manner that the lines and shapes seem to move when you stare too long at a painting. The artist intends to confuse the viewer with narrow, parallel lines or even-sized circles. Sometimes, the artist suggests depth, a third dimension, as the eye is carried along parallel lines to the middle of a jumping composition. In Illus. 159, an Op Art composition was achieved by means of the crayon relief technique. The light, subtle, delicate, timid, regular pattern of the mesh is richly set off by the bold reds of the circular design which covers them.

String Drawings in Crayon Relief

String is a line. And by using it to enclose shapes, you may "draw" attractive forms on newsprint. Young children will enjoy arranging their string-line into representational shapes, while older students and adults might prefer scribble drawings. Let the string wind about and overlap upon itself on a hard surface. Place your paper above the laid-out string, and stroke with the side

Illus. 162. The final stage of the string-line drawing, with the plain shapes and patterned areas embellished with red, yellow, chartreuse and black crayon.

of a peeled crayon. Some of the shapes created with the string-line may be accented with textural materials from the "texture box."

Illus. 163 (above). A long piece of string has been arranged to form a double flower blossom design. The peeled side of a black crayon colors the raised design.

Illus. 164 (below). The sheet of newsprint has been moved about one inch, so that a double image appears when crayon is applied again. The design could be carried further by adding colors and patterns within the shapes established by the double-line image.

Illus. 165. The figure of an Alpine yodeler is constructed upon a paper cone. The relief technique has been used to decorate his trousers and suspenders.

Decorating 3-Dimensional Objects

The crayon relief technique may be applied to paper and cloth to create clothes and decorations for 3-dimensional figures. Illus. 165 and 166 were constructed from paper over a narrow cone, which was fashioned from paper.

The male figure in Illus. 165 was made of red construction paper crayon rubbed over a plastic doily to create the trousers, hat and suspenders. White crayon was rubbed over the red construction paper to create the patterns seen in his clothing.

In Illus. 166, ever smaller circles of newsprint received their patterns by means of the crayon relief process, using a plastic doily as an underlay. A hole was cut with a scissor in the middle of each paper circle which forms the skirt. Certain shapes of the doily relief pattern were filled with solid color, visible in the bottom ruffles. Other textured papers were cut and pasted to the cone to form the hat and gloves.

Patterns may also be applied to plain cloth by means of the crayon relief technique. Young seamstresses will enjoy using their own crayoned patterns when designing doll clothes or garments for a puppet.

Many exciting uses for the crayon relief technique will come to mind as you explore the technique. And a strong feeling for texture and pattern will develop as you apply the technique in many ways.

Illus. 166. This young lady in 3-D has been made by attaching paper shapes to a cone which is also constructed from paper. The relief technique adorns the skirt, hat, blouse, and gloves.

CHAPTER EIGHT

Exploring with Melted Wax Crayons

The Crayon Encaustic Technique (Painting with Melted Wax)

By applying heat to crayon, a whole new series of avenues is opened for artistic expression and exploration. Wax crayons, when heated, turn liquid, making a medium that can be thin and flowing, or thick and textural, according to the amount of applied heat.

The practice of painting with melted wax colors is by no means a recent one. The Egyptians used this so-called encaustic or burning-in technique to decorate their mummy cases and to create wall paintings. The early Egyptian wax paintings have remained magnificently well preserved through many centuries because the Egyptian climate is warm and dry. But the Egyptians did not use crayons for their paintings—they had a special secret formula for the wax which has been forgotten and lost with the passage of time.

Melting Method #1: The Candle

When experimenting with the encaustic technique, you might heat your crayon by holding it briefly over a lighted candle. The crayon should be quickly applied to your chosen surface before the molten wax has a chance to harden. Place the painting close to the candle flame so that the moving air has little chance to cool the crayon as it makes its brief trip from the flame to the painting surface. (See Illus. 167.)

Illus. 167. Painted with wax crayon melted above the flame of a candle, this clown shows up vividly on black construction paper. The melting crayon was applied quickly and frequently to the surface. The heated end of the wax crayon was applied to the paper in a rolling motion so that the melted wax came from all sides of the crayon's end. After each rolling application, the crayon was reheated.

To create a thick impasto, allow the crayon to cool a little more than usual on its way from candle to surface. Minute gobs of melted wax will create a surface which suggests the tesserae of a mosaic.

Unusual crayon colors such as gold, silver, flesh, pale green and blue-grey enrich the encaustic painting.

Although the candle is an appropriate source of heat for the adult artist, this method leaves something to be desired for the classroom. The dangers involved when students work over an open flame are immediately apparent. In many instances, the use of the candle is in opposition to local fire regulations. Crayons may be safely melted for class use in a number of other ways, however, as we shall see.

Illus. 169. Crayons may be melted in the separate compartments of a muffin tin. A 100-watt bulb provides the heat.

Method #2: Muffin Tin and Light Bulb

Place broken, peeled crayons in a muffin tin (Illus. 169). Be sure to separate the colors properly so that crayons of only one color are placed within each muffin tin compartment. Mixed colors often turn a dull grey when

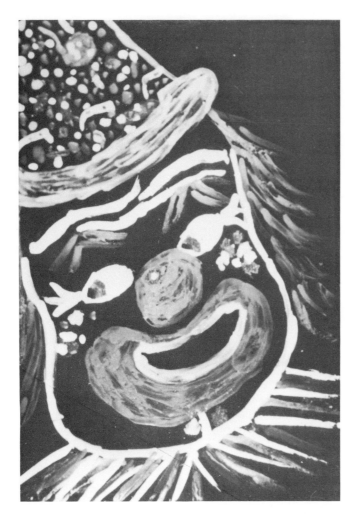

Illus. 170. Using crayons melted in tin cans surrounded by boiling water, the artist had a highly liquid and flowing medium to brush on for his clown.

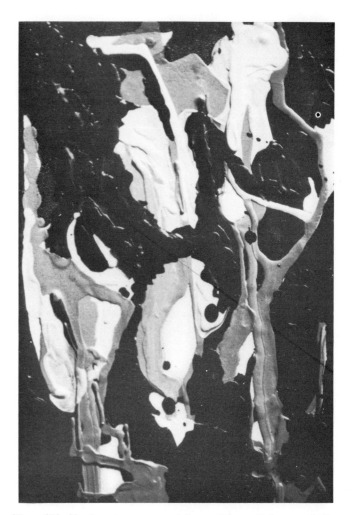

Illus. 171. No brush was used here. The artist, an adult, poured molten wax from fruit juice cans onto a cardboard surface to create "The Three Figures." Hot pads were used to protect his fingers when handling the cans. When cool, the cardboard backing began to warp. To remedy this, the painting was placed in a hot oven and heated at a low temperature, causing the cardboard to return to its original flat state.

melted together. Place the muffin tin atop a rectangular-shaped tin can (or any open-top metal box) large enough for a wired 100-watt bulb to be placed inside it. The heat of the bulb (when switched on) will effectively melt the crayons lying above. This method is safe for melting crayons within the classroom.

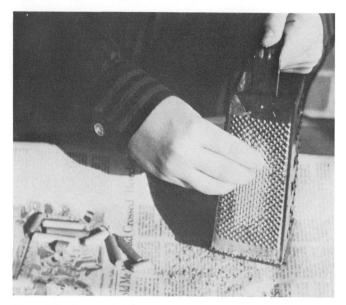

Illus. 172. A vegetable grater is a useful tool for grating crayons to prepare them for melting in place.

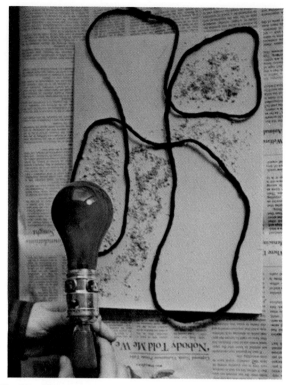

Illus. 173. Position the gratings on the chosen background surface, using a glued piece of yarn to separate the areas. Then, using a lighted bulb, held close to the shavings, melt them.

Method #3: Tin Cans and Hot Water

Crayons may also be melted in small tin cans, such as orange juice cans. Place the cans in a shallow pan of water. An electric hot plate or any single burner may be your source of heat. Heat the pan until the water reaches the boiling point and until the crayons have completely melted. Then turn off the heat and remove the pan from the stove, using pot holders. Pads of newspaper should be placed beneath the pan of hot water so as to prevent damage to the table top. The hot water will keep the wax in a molten stage for quite some time. Using a stiff bristle brush, apply the melted wax to your chosen surface.

The hot water brings the wax to a far hotter stage than a candle flame. The wax becomes more watery and flows onto a surface like paint. You can readily see how flowing the strokes of color are in Illus. 170 compared with the rough texture of Illus. 167.

Method #4: Sunshine and Turpentine

If working on a hot summer day, simply place your crayons and muffin tin in the hot sun for a few moments. This method is the safest for children of the primary grades. Add a small amount of turpentine to quicken the melting process. Youngsters can use a stiff bristle brush, tongue depressor or palette knife for applying the melted wax to the chosen surface.

Method #5: Light Bulb and Crayon Shavings

A convenient and messless melting method requires the artist to first create crayon shavings by rubbing peeled crayons over a vegetable grater (Illus. 172) or shaving them with a scissors blade. These shavings, placed on paper, melt when a lighted bulb is moved close above the crayon shavings (Illus. 173). Layer upon layer of shavings may be added. Each application of heat can fuse a layer onto the background until a rich impasto is obtained.

In Illus. 173, a fifth-grade student began his wax painting by arranging a piece of black yarn in a looping pattern and glueing it to a sheet of tagboard. Within a few of the shapes, he placed shavings to be melted by the light bulb. Later, shavings were deposited in other shapes outlined by overlapping yarn.

Method #6: A Crayon Sandwich

This approach involves using tagboard, crayon shavings and a hot iron. Shavings of various colors are arranged in the desired pattern on one sheet of tagboard. Then they are sandwiched in by a second sheet of tagboard placed on top. A hot flatiron is run over the top sheet to melt the shavings. The iron may be used on *both* sides of the crayon sandwich to assure thorough and uniform melting. The two sheets are pulled apart while the wax is still in a molten state. The heat will have caused the shavings to fuse and flow together, forming what may well be an accidental design. When pulling the two sheets of tagboard apart, you will discover that you have two sheets each containing the same color areas. You have two surfaces to experiment on.

Work beyond the accidental stage and don't rely on accident alone. In carrying the design further, you might use a fine brush and India ink to add a line design or to accent certain parts of the design. Use a matchstick dipped in India ink for a free spontaneous line design. Try a dark colored crayon to add color and line. Or, apply more melted crayon with a brush or by the approach called Method #5.

If you want a representational landscape, plan the location of your colored shavings more carefully before melting them. Colors for trees, mountains, sky and grass may be chosen and placed in certain specific areas. After

Illus. 174. To move beyond the accidental stage of the sandwich method, red and blue crayon shavings were carefully arranged to suggest flowers, and green shavings to suggest lacy foliage. Heat was carefully applied. When the areas came out textured, India ink was used to draw in delicate stems and leaf veins. The product has the subtle color quality of a watercolor.

the melting process, line and pattern may be added to define tree trunks, fence posts and other objects. If the colors have gotten a bit out of control, they may be covered with a different layer of melted wax, applied with the brush. As in oil painting, all mistakes can be corrected easily.

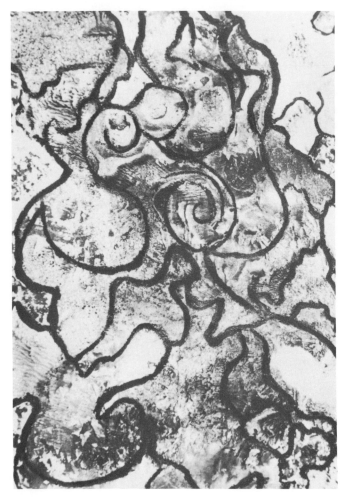

Illus. 177. While melted black crayon has been applied to all background areas, the texture of the burlap comes peeking through, creating an interesting textural pattern.

Illus. 175. Coarse shavings make textured designs with Method #6. The smooth and rough areas of this work complement each other. A black wax crayon was melted and applied with a brush on the design to create the heavy, defining lines.

Illus. 176. An electric palette with eight cups for melting crayons. A third-grade student in Los Alamos, New Mexico, uses stiff bristle brushes and cotton swabs for executing an encaustic. (Photo by John Agee.)

94

Choosing Background Material

A wide variety of surfaces can be used to paint upon with the encaustic technique. For thin layers of wax, paper will serve as an adequate background. For thick applications you might wish to use matboard, cardboard, chipboard, wallboard, plywood, plasterboard or insulating tiles. As for cloths, many can serve. For extra support, any thin or thick cloth might be glued to cardboard or another hard material.

Burlap is the most textural cloth and holds the wax beautifully. Illus. 177 and 178 were both created on natural burlap of a tan color.

Black felt provides a fine background in Illus. 180, as the crayon colors are especially vivid and beautiful against jet black. (Black velvet also provides exciting shading effects.) Observe the shading effects achieved in the green leaves and the vase. The right side of the vase faces the source of light and is, therefore, lighter in value.

Melted wax adheres to glass surprisingly well. Leave some of the glass transparent to complement the opaque wax portions of your design. The Hallowe'en design

Illus. 178. Painted with melted wax on burlap, this rectangular motif echoes the style of Mondrian, the modern Dutch painter. Variety comes in color and size of the repeated rectangles.

Illus. 179. Melted crayon wax has been painted on a sheet of transparent glass to create this Hallowe'en design.

pictured in Illus. 179, complete with pumpkin, ghost, fence, stars and moon, has a black sheet of construction paper placed behind the transparent glass to deepen the murky effect of the night and to set off the Hallowe'en symbols.

But beforehand, white crayon was applied to the green background papers to suggest the hills and outlines and to define the distant evergreen trees.

Surface Textures

To get a variety of interesting surface textures for a melted wax crayon painting, you may vary the thickness of wax you apply. In some areas, build up the wax almost to a 3-dimensional state, leaving surrounding areas thin and flat.

To get a shine, polish the wax surface of the finished painting with a soft cloth. The raised portions will literally glow, giving a pronounced contrast with the duller recessed areas of wax.

A wax painting is greatly enhanced when sprayed with a commercial fixative. The colors of wax when fixed

Illus. 181. Melted wax completely covers the glass background of this design.

Melted wax completely covers the glass background and forms a geometric design in Illus. 181. Three colors—yellow, orange and green—have been carefully balanced and repeated throughout the composition. Melted wax and cut paper are combined to form the Christmas tree scene in Illus. 182. An old glassed picture frame with the original picture removed was used. Painting right on the glass with melted crayon wax, the artist created the tree, light bulbs, snowflakes and snow. Two shades of green construction paper were placed behind the transparent glass to form a base for distant hills and evergreen trees.

suggest the quality of an oil painting—that is, the colors become more brilliant and shiny.

Mixing Melted Colors

When using melted wax crayons, it is possible to mix your own colors as with a painter's palette. Different proportions of yellow and blue crayons can create shades of green when melted together. Red and blue crayons produce various purples. Yellow and red create hues of orange. You should always place the lightest of the colors in your container first, as the dark colors are stronger and override the light colors.

Dot Pictures

The technique of painting with dots of melted crayon, called Pointillism (see page 20), is another means of creating the appearance of new hues. Minute yellow dots placed next to minute blue dots will produce a green hue when the area is viewed from a distance.

Illus. 182 (above). The Christmas tree, snowflakes, and snow are all painted in wax right on the glass belonging to an old picture frame. The two shades of green are achieved by placing white-crayoned green construction paper behind the glass to suggest the distant mountains and evergreen trees.

Illus. 183 (left). Melted crayons and a Q-tip are used by the young artist to apply small dabs of color onto a paper background.

When exploring Pointillism, the Q-tip, available from the drugstore, is the most appropriate tool. In Illus. 183, the young artist dips the end of her Q-tip into various compartments of her muffin tin which contains melted wax crayon. In Illus. 184, after small dabs of wax have been neatly applied to a sheet of tagboard you can see the finished design, just as Seurat might have done it!

Adding a Color Wash

On occasion you might enhance your paintings by adding a wash consisting of transparent watercolor, thinned tempera or dissolved water crayon. A dark wash will cause dark flecks to show on the crayoned areas, suggesting a hand-blocked effect. Also, a dark wash will cover any unwaxed portion of the background, provided the background consists of paper. Painting on dark background areas this way will frequently accentuate and enliven the bold, warm, intense colors of wax.

A brush was used in Illus. 186 to paint the repeat design in yellow melted wax. The background paper had been

Illus. 184. With the Q-tip the young girl of Illus. 183 has executed an example of Pointillism in the style of Seurat. She has placed small, vibrant dots of different colors next to each other to form a tree, house and sun— objects she finds easy to portray.

Illus. 185. The surfaces of the vases in this painting glitter with a shimmering glow of dotted crayon paint. Observe all of the subtle gradations of value which are realized in this painting.

Illus. 186. Using a stiff bristle brush, the artist painted yellow molten wax "animals" on paper.

Illus. 187. Adding a wash of dark blue tempera changes the whole character of the painting and adds a bubbly design on the yellow wax areas.

creased so that the vertical and horizontal folds could aid the artist in organizing his repeated motif. Then dark blue tempera was painted over the melted crayon design (Illus. 187). Observe how vividly the colored wax now appears against this darker background. Observe also the interesting bubbles of dark paint which were left to decorate the solid areas of yellow wax.

Applying Melted Crayon To 3-Dimensional Objects

The encaustic technique need not be limited to 2-dimensional surfaces. You will enjoy decorating papier-mâché objects with melted wax—a papier-mâché-covered balloon, for example, or a fantastic animal created from wire and papier-mâché. Or you might

Illus. 188. A papier mâché poodle is decorated with streaks of crayon wax dripped onto its surface.

Illus. 189. Melted crayon may be used to decorate 3-dimensional objects. Narrow strips of dry newspaper were covered with white library paste and wound around a pipe-cleaner frame to create the papier mâché animal.

Illus. 190. Brown and yellow stripes of molten wax were then painted on the animal form so as to decorate it colorfully. Observe that humps appear upon the animal's back in the decorated example, but not when undecorated. These humps consist of solid wax. They were sculptured on the animal's back after the wax had cooled to the stage where it could be comfortably handled.

decorate a paper sculptured figure with thin layers of melted wax. Tagboard can be used to create a rather sturdy 3-dimensional object, as tagboard holds wax beautifully.*

* Suggestions and methods for creating 3-dimensional paper objects may be found in Prof. Alkema's book "Creative Paper Crafts in Color" (Sterling Publishing Co., Inc., New York, and Oak Tree Press Co., Ltd., London).

In Illus. 188, the poodle's body was constructed from a tube of rolled newspaper. Papier-mâché strips were used to build up the head, ears and legs. Red, white and green crayons were held next to the flame of a candle and allowed to drip down on the poodle form.

Melted Crayon Transfers

It is an easy matter to make a transfer design of any of your melted crayon paintings. Place a clean sheet of newsprint upon the design and iron it with a hot flatiron. Heat causes some of the wax of the painting to transfer onto the newsprint. The exact image of the original design (in reverse) will be seen transferred to the sheet of newsprint.

Melted Crayon Window Transparencies

Sunlight from a window causes the melted crayon colors of a simulated stained glass transparency to glow intensely. The transparencies may be made by pressing crayon shavings between two sheets of wax paper using a hot flatiron. (Do not pull apart.) Black lines may be painted later on the surface of the wax paper, using India ink, to suggest the lead tracings of a stained glass window. Strips of black construction paper may also be used.

In Illus. 191 the window transparency was created by

Illus. 191. Crayon shavings have been melted between two sheets of wax paper to provide the transparent colors seen in this simulated stained glass window.

Illus. 192. Colored fish and other forms were cut from sandwiches of wax paper and shavings and placed with blue and green crayon shavings between two other sheets of wax paper. The blue shavings were used to suggest ocean waters. A hot iron then pressed and fused all inner parts to the outer wax paper layers.

Illus. 193. All colors were kept pure and unmixed by placing only red shavings between two sheets of wax paper, blue shavings between another two sheets of wax paper, etc. Shapes were then cut from the various wax paper sandwiches and pasted behind "windows" cut from black background paper. The flaming red border was made from heated sheets of wax paper which had red, orange and white shavings between them.

Illus. 194. String was glued to a sheet of wax paper to create the three daisy blossoms, and blue crayon shavings were sprinkled within each petal. Black construction paper was cut to fit the background. Next, black construction paper was folded back and forth to create an oriental fan, and shapes were cut away, along the folds of the fan. When unfolded, it became the open pattern of diamond shapes. Then, a second sheet of wax paper was placed over everything and fused to the other sheet with a hot iron, sealing all within the two layers.

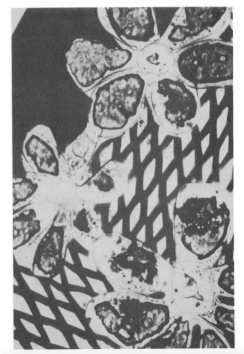

cutting interesting shapes from a sheet of black construction paper, using a single-edge razor blade. The narrow black strips suggest the stained glass window's tracings. Colored shavings were melted between two sheets of wax paper, and the sealed sheets were placed behind the openings.

You might wish to enhance your window transparencies by inserting materials between the sheets of wax paper in addition to the shavings. String, yarn and thread, colored construction paper forms, and paper cut-outs will provide a pleasing opaque contrast to the transparent areas. Exciting effects are also obtained when the crayon shavings are pressed between sheets of colored tissue paper instead of wax paper.

Tissue paper was used to create Illus. 195. A sheet of construction paper was folded and cut, then unfolded to reveal the butterfly shape. Yellow and white tissue paper shapes were pasted beneath the black paper tracings. Red, yellow and multi-color shavings were then sprinkled upon the shapes and a large sheet of white tissue was placed over everything. Once the sandwich of the two layers of tissue was ready, a warm iron was applied to partially melt the shavings. Since back-and-forth movements of the iron would tear the delicate tissue paper, the iron was laid upon an area, raised and repositioned until the entire surface had been heated.

Illus. 196. Dabs of melted crayon were applied to broken pieces of sheet glass to create this musical mobile. Nylon thread inserted through drilled holes supports the various pieces of glass.

Melted Crayon Mobiles

The extra heavy wax paper designed for use in the freezer also has possibilities. Hanging mobiles may be made from shapes cut from two sheets of this paper that

Illus. 195. Tissue paper transparency. (See text.)

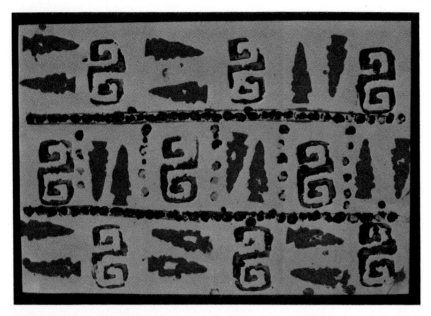

Illus. 197. The smooth surfaces of several raw potatoes were carved into three motifs, and then used as blocks to print in melted crayon on yellow construction paper.

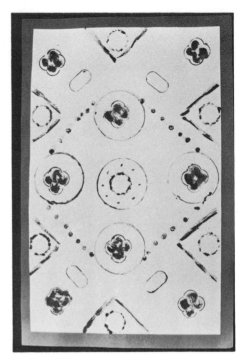

Illus. 198. Various household gadgets were used to print in melted wax upon paper.

have been pressed (using a flatiron) with crayon shavings and string secured between. To create 3-dimensional forms, two shapes may be inserted within one another, by means of vertical slits—one half-way down from the top, and the other shape's slit running from the bottom up. Rick-rack, Christmas glitter, buttons, etc., may be used to decorate the surfaces of the mobile.

Printing with Melted Wax Crayons

Add one part cooking oil to four parts melted wax crayon to make the wax conducive to printing. Cooking oil will not burn at high temperatures.

A vegetable, such as potato, onion, carrot or turnip, provides an excellent printing tool. Slice the vegetable into two parts, to leave two flat surfaces. With a knife, make your design by cutting away the parts of the surface which are *not* to print. Dip the printing surface into the liquid wax mixture, lift it out and press it onto a sheet of paper. Repeat the process until a rhythmic design is established. If you want evenly spaced areas, fold the paper prior to printing to obtain creased outlined rectangles.

Various household gadgets are fun to use as printing tools. Common articles, such as spools, clothespins, or scrap wood blocks may be used. Lids from jars, a plastic fork, wooden spoons, ice cream sticks and a bent piece of metal are other printing devices. Illus. 198 was made with a band-aid box, tin can, gauze, pencil eraser and the end of a brush roller. With a little ingenuity you will find many cast-off items with pleasing shapes to become printing plates.

CHAPTER NINE

Exploring with the Crayon Resist Technique

Crayoning by the resist technique will be an enjoyable experience for you—whether you are of nursery school age or 80 years old. The height of excitement is reached when you apply a wash of contrasting color over your crayon lines, patterns and shapes. How rewarding it is to watch how the wax and oil crayon markings resist the wash, how the lovely intense, brilliant colors sing out against their background, how unity of color is brought about by the wash, and how black flecks give the crayoned areas a hand-blocked effect.

Illus. 199 (upper right). Mary, a college student, draws a design on manila paper, using wax crayons. Oil crayons might likewise have been used as they too have resisting qualities. Note that Mary's design consists of solid shapes of color within color. Open areas of pattern, small dots and other figures might have been added.

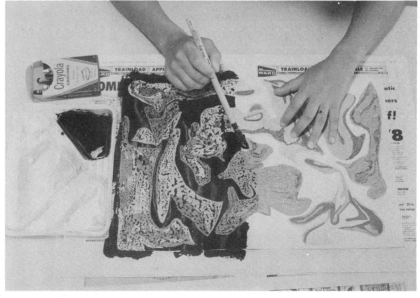

Illus. 200 (right). Mary now applies her wash of black tempera. Observe how distinctly her crayon shapes resist the dark wash. Observe also the attractive, spotted effect which occurs when the black paint is brushed over the crayon shapes. The paint leaves little bubbles on the waxy surface, creating a textural pattern.

Illus. 201. The drawing on manila paper made by Pamela, a fifth-grade student, differs from Mary's in that it is more open, with fewer solid color shapes, and more patterned areas. The black tempera wash causes all of the colorful patterns to "pop" through by contrast in value. Children call this "black magic."

Approach #1: Dark Wash over Light Colors

In the first of two basic approaches the artist draws light colored lines, patterns and/or solid shapes upon light colored paper, using wax crayons or oil pastels. Next he paints a dark colored wash over it. The wax lines resist the dark wash, but the paper absorbs it where its surface is not covered with wax crayon markings.

The drawings and paintings on these two pages were all created by fifth-grade pupils. The students enjoyed experimenting with different papers as each paper affected the crayon drawing and the applied wash somewhat differently. They found that white on white shows up in this process and that the brightest, boldest, warmest crayon colors give the most pronounced contrast to the black wash.

Illus. 202. Robert, another fifth-grader, combines representational forms with abstract shapes in an interesting way.

Illus. 203. Tim (grade 5) introduced many solid shapes of crayon color in his design, so that the wash darkened a limited area only. The warm red and yellow colors appear rich against the background. The red border effectively repeats the dominant color.

Illus. 204. Rhonda, a fifth-grader, created a formally balanced crayon resist design. A large amount of bright color glows through the black resisting wash.

Illus. 205. Bonnie (grade 5) was not hesitant to place white crayon on white paper since she understood that the black wash would cause the white crayon markings to show up vividly.

Illus. 206. Mike (grade 5) made his crayoned red and grey solids combine beautifully with black shapes. Solid shapes of color contribute to the bold abstract design and minimize the space available for delicate patterned areas.

Preliminary Suggestions
For Executing Crayon Resists

At this point, it might be well to point out that occasionally the crayon resist technique leads to discouragement and disappointment. To prevent failures, the classroom teacher might follow this advice. First of all, encourage students to press very hard with their crayons. A weak, timid line simply will not resist an opaque wash. Encourage children to cover all "pores" of the paper when applying their crayon colors. Second, encourage pupils to experiment with their chosen wash and crayons on scrap paper before attempting to complete their prized drawings. The student may have to add more water or more tempera before the wash covers and is resisted effectively. Different tempera colors manufactured by the same firm do not work equally well, and identical colors from different manufacturers will differ too. On occasion, tempera will work best if it is first applied as a thin, transparent wash; when dry, a second coat of the same wash is applied; a third wash might be needed to achieve an opaque background.

Certain brands of crayons differ in their ability to resist a wash. Some colors become lost beneath tempera. Test first. It is most disconcerting for children to spend a great amount of time and effort on a crayon drawing, only to lose it beneath a sea of paint.

Do not scrub wax drawings when applying the wash. Move the brush gently in a single direction, just once, over the wax. If an area is lost beneath the wash, a dry, clean brush may

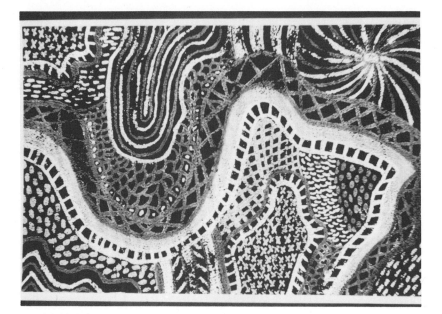

Illus. 207. Biology was correlated with art in an imaginative, creative, uncopied way in this and the next crayon resist illustration by junior high school students.

Illus. 208. This and Illus. 207 were created by junior high school students inspired by the study of stained biological specimens viewed through a microscope. Both students correlated their new-found knowledge with their favorite technique in art. The microscope enables artists of all ages to discover many new patterns, shapes, and forms.

Illus. 209 and 210. Black and orange combinations are winners every time. Curved, snake-like formations are closely knit to form a lovely, rhythmic design in Illus. 209. Yellow and white areas, next to the dominant orange and black colors, cause the total design to vibrate with color. In Illus. 210, aqua blue colors are repeated throughout the composition and provide a cool relief to the warm pervading hues. Observe the many beautiful patterns repeated throughout this design.

be used to pick up the excess paint. Or, dab the area with facial tissue. Dried tempera may be scratched off a wax-crayoned line or shape by using your fingernail, if the tempera has not resisted properly.

Illus. 211. Line is the dominant design element portrayed here. The border beautifully repeats both the light and medium blues found within the crayon resist design. This and Illus. 212 through 217 are creations of adult art education students at Grand Valley State College and Michigan State University.

Illus. 213. The block print effect, caused by the bubbles of paint deposited during the black wash application, contribute much to the textural beauty of this design.

Illus. 212. Solid, patterned shapes, irregular, unusual and textural in nature, fill the composition. Common shapes are avoided.

If a crayon resist design has turned out beautifully except for one area which did not resist properly, cut the area out with a scissors and place a new sheet of paper beneath the opening, pasting it to the rear side of your drawing. Using crayon, again draw your design over the new area, continuing the lines established on the original drawing. When finished, apply your wash to the newly crayoned area so that it matches the surrounding parts of the original design.

Papers and Tempera

Manila paper works well, but you will enjoy using other papers as well. Colored construction paper, when used, can change the whole tone and mood of a work, especially when the wash is somewhat transparent.

Tagboard, being hard and smooth, provides a different final effect from manila and construction paper. The edges of the crayon markings appear somewhat sharper after the wash has been added. And since the wash penetrates the tagboard to a lesser extent, the crayon markings stand out boldly against the background. When using tagboard, you have no "pores" to fill since the upper surface is hard and smooth. Consequently, you face less chance of losing crayon markings beneath the wash. The wax builds up more easily on the surface of

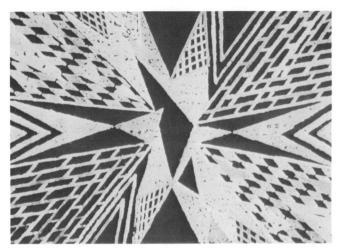

Illus. 214. An explosion in a shingle factory? This work has a most explosive quality. Everything seems to be bursting from the central focal point. The radial balance and movement of the work demand more than a passing glance.

Illus. 216. The design is both simple and charming and illustrates that the crayon resist technique need not always be executed in a detailed manner. The childlike quality of this work makes it a fitting addition to a nursery room or child's bedroom.

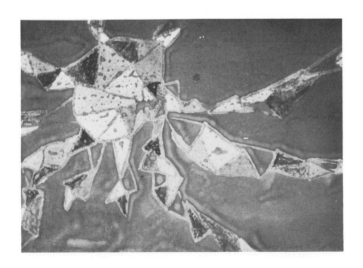

Illus. 215. The work of a sixth-grade student using a dark blue wash.

Illus. 217. The colors, patterns and shapes here are beautiful to behold. The pinks, greens and reds sing out in glorious color against the dark background. The shapes cause the imagination to race with ideas. Is this a butterfly with symmetrical wings? The front of an insect's face? A strange bird from another planet? Or is it just an abstract design to be appreciated for its unusual properties?

Illus. 218. When using the dark over light crayon resist approach, it is fun to experiment with tempera and watercolor washes other than black. Sometimes a dark blue better complements the chosen colors of wax and oil crayons. This creation by a sixth-grade student shows how a dark blue tempera wash was used to resist the bright, warm crayon colors.

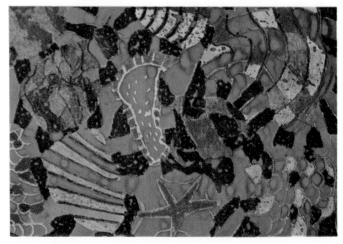

the paper. You do not have to press your crayon as hard to achieve a well-covered line of wax.

Shelf paper, brown wrapping paper and wallpaper may also be used with interesting results. Even a sheet of newspaper containing fine print may be used. The lines of print provide young students with a guide in the placement of lines, patterns and texture. All printed matter disappears once the wash has been added. Only the crayon colors are visible against the contrasting wash.

Tempera paint mixed to the consistency of thin cream provides a suitable wash but students will also enjoy experimenting with various hues of transparent watercolor and water crayon to achieve other interesting effects.

Approach #2: Light Wash over Dark Colors

In employing this approach, dark crayon colors are applied to a sheet of dark colored paper. Once the drawing is complete, a paint, light in color, is washed over the crayon markings to achieve contrast. Illus. 219 demonstrates the interesting results obtained by using this approach.

Illus. 220. The total color range here is light in value, because a light rose color was chosen for the background paper. Dark blue and pink crayon colors were applied before the milky white tempera wash. The color of background paper will affect the whole mood of a crayon resist drawing. Try light washes other than white to produce unusual effects.

Illus. 219. Dark crayons applied to dark colored paper are painted over with a light colored wash to achieve these interesting effects with a drawing inspired by Mother Nature's plant forms.

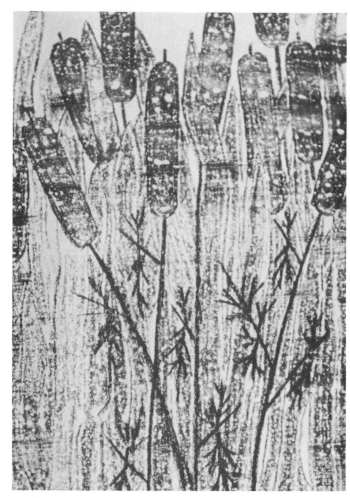

Illus. 221. Dark maroon and dark green were applied to a small sheet of black construction paper. A white, milky tempera wash was then painted over the design. The lovely flowered tree and rolling hills seem to be placed in a wintry, frosty environment.

Illus. 222. Cattails provide the subject matter for this drawing. The lower half seemed too uniform and uninteresting after the wash had been added. Consequently, black crayon was used to add a few stems and foliage to break the monotony.

114

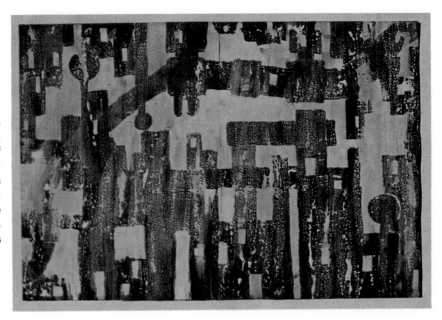

Illus. 223. Dark blue, red and brown crayons were applied to a blue sheet of construction paper. Open patterns are avoided in favor of solid rectangular shapes outlined by strong vertical and horizontal edges. Diagonal lines are almost completely avoided. The milky, transparent white tempera wash reveals some of the construction paper's color and deposits an interesting texture upon the waxy areas of solid color.

In both approaches, the artist is seeking a contrast of color. If you are a classroom teacher you may wish to discuss methods for achieving contrast more fully with your pupils: "Would you think of painting a black dog lying on a coal pile? How about painting a white rabbit hopping on a snowbank? Why not? Because both the dog and the rabbit would be difficult to see. The backgrounds would be too similar to the animals in color and value, and there would be a lack of contrast. In our crayon resist work we are interested in achieving contrast. However, we will want to achieve this contrast during our last step, when the wash is added. So, don't be afraid to use dark colors on dark paper since a light wash will later provide contrast. But never use a crayon hue that is identical to the color of the wash."

Illus. 224. A strong horizontal movement is achieved by means of curved lines and patterns moving from left to right. There is plenty of variety in this design as solid shapes are juxtaposed with open patterns consisting of diagonal lines, circles, and dots. Blue crayon was applied to dark blue construction paper, topped by a white tempera wash. The bubbly design, most visible in the solid wax areas, was caused by the white tempera wash, and effectively echoes the dot and circle patterns repeated within the design.

Illus. 225. A realistic-shaped fish displaying many different patterns and colors was rendered on brown construction paper with warm crayon colors. A tan, almost transparent wash was applied over the crayon lines. Black India ink was applied last to darken and accent some of the tail patterns and to outline the fish.

Illus. 226. A variegated background was created by applying two coats of a white transparent tempera wash over this crayon drawing on green background paper. The second coat caused certain areas to appear whiter, more opaque. The flower blossom petals have many coats of wash, causing them to display an impenetrable white.

Applying a Variegated Wash

When executing a crayon resist design, you might wish to apply crayon and watercolor or tempera in a succession of stages. After the first wash has been applied over crayon, you can draw upon the painted surface, adding more crayon markings. Also, you can later add another wash to your work. Perhaps you would like to add a second wash just to certain areas, causing parts of the background to become darker (or lighter) and more opaque.

In Illus. 228, a thin, white transparent tempera wash was painted over the crayon colors on a green background sheet of construction paper. When dry, a second application of the white transparent wash was added to certain areas of the background so that these areas became more opaque, more chalky white. Thus, a variegated tone was achieved. As for the flower blossoms, you

will observe that as many as four applications of white tempera wash were applied to some of the petals so that they became a pure, opaque white.

Illus. 227. The yellow butterflies appear brighter than the background because they have been painted many times with the transparent yellow tempera wash.

Illus. 228.

Illus. 229. In this and Illus. 228, transparent washes were generously applied. The drawings were held at a 45-degree angle while drying so that the paint could collect near the wax lines.

Much the same approach was used to execute the butterfly design in Illus. 227. Certain butterfly shapes were given extra coats of the transparent yellow wash to make them stand out more vividly.

The dramatic tree in Illus. 229 was drawn on grey construction paper. A watery transparent tempera wash was generously applied. While still wet, the design was held at a 45-degree angle to dry. The slanted position caused the transparent wash to collect along the edges of each branch, thereby creating opaque puddles of white color. A similar approach was used to create Illus. 228.

In Illus. 230, a different effect was achieved by using thick tempera and a stiff bristle brush. No attempt was made to hide the brush strokes, leaving both thin and thick areas of white paint, which contribute to a frosty, wintry feeling.

Special Effects

A variety of effects will be obtained with the crayon resist technique if you are willing to experiment. Sometimes it is fun to violate the known methods and see what happens. Suppose dark colors were applied to light paper, which is then covered with a light wash instead of the usual dark wash. Illus. 232 shows you what happens. The thin white tempera wash allows some of the manila background color to come through in places. The white

Illus. 230. Red and black crayon shapes were drawn on maroon construction paper. A thick white tempera wash, about the consistency of light cream, was applied with a stiff bristle brush so as to leave stroke marks, thereby creating a variegated effect.

Illus. 231. The crayon resist technique provides one of the most suitable means for suggesting a winter blizzard. A white wash painted with diagonal strokes over a solid dark blue sky will create a remarkable illusion of falling snow. Here a fifth-grade student in the Kalamazoo (Mich.) public schools has used the resist technique in his "Winter Fun." Slanting white snow seems to be falling out of a dark blue sky and over the colorful garments worn by the tobogganers.

Illus. 232. Experimentation will lead to special effects with the crayon resist technique. Both approaches were violated here, and dark crayon was applied to light paper, covered by a light wash—with pleasing results.

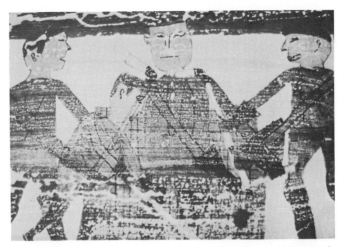

Illus. 233. A sixth-grade student painted a white wash over his three hockey players so as to place them in a wintry environment. (Courtesy of the Kalamazoo, Mich., Public Schools.)

bubble pattern is seen atop the repeated octopus motif, but not on the background. And all crayoned shapes show up vividly since dark crayons were used in the first place.

Sometimes it is the bubbles of paint, the texture, the hand-blocked effect that most enhance a crayon drawing. You can get the desired effect in certain designated areas, but not all over. Apply the wash to cover solid crayoned areas only, and not the unwaxed background.

Falling raindrops may best be shown in representational scenes by means of the crayon resist technique. A light grey wash painted diagonally over a dark blue sky will create a realistic illusion of a summer rain. For falling snow, use a white wash.

Combining Techniques

For greater experimentation, why not combine the crayon resist technique with other crayon techniques explored in this book? Textures and patterns may be

Illus. 234. The crayon stencil technique was used to apply the red and pink repeat pattern. A blue tempera was washed over the crayoned shapes.

Illus. 235. Drawing with a ball-point pen on the opposite side of a heavily crayoned sheet of paper transferred the basic design to tagboard which was then covered with black tempera.

applied to newsprint by means of the crayon relief technique, for example. A wash of contrasting value might be just the thing needed to reveal the intricate, subtle lines of a delicate crayon relief pattern. Or how about combining the encaustic and the resist techniques? You need not worry about filling in the paper's "pores" if you use melted crayon. When dry and cool, thick and thin lines and solid areas of melted wax will positively resist the subsequent wash, even if the tempera paint is extra thick.

The crayon resist and the crayon stencil techniques may also be combined as in Illus. 234.

sheet #1 newsprint A

sheet #2 tagboard C B

Illus. 236.

Crayon Resist Transfer Designs

Here is a unique and unusual method for using the crayon resist technique which you may want to try.

The top sheet of newsprint and the bottom sheet of tagboard should be the same size. Color side B of your newsprint with one light crayon color, such as white, yellow, orange, etc. Cover it completely, so that none of the paper's surface shows through. Place Sheet #1 upon Sheet #2 so that sides B and C face one another. While the sheets are firmly together, draw a line design upon surface A, using a sharp ball-point pen. Work on a hard surface and press hard so that the line design inked on

Illus. 237. Described in the text.

Illus. 238. Described in the text.

Watercolor was the medium used in Illus. 237 and 238. A thin watery medium was first washed over the tagboard's entire surface and allowed to dry. Next, second and third coats of watercolor were applied to certain shapes designated by the wax lines, to make them stand out more boldly.

Using Cloth and Crumpled Paper

Apply melted or unmelted crayon to sections of an old cloth sheet, then soak it in a dark-colored cold-water dye. When dry, add more areas of wax, if desired.

Try coloring the entire surface of newsprint with light color crayon shapes, perhaps outlined with black. Soak the crayoned paper in clear water and crumple the sheet in your hands. Spread out and, when dry, apply a dark watercolor wash over the surface. This will sink into the crinkles of the paper, creating a texture which suggests leather. The wash will resist all other areas. An interesting transfer design may be made of the drawing by pressing the colored surface (with a warm iron) against another sheet of paper.

surface A will cause the crayon on surface B to deposit a wax line on surface C. The deposited wax line design will be barely visible if white crayon was placed on surface B. (Surface C is also light in value.) Next, dilute a water crayon so that the paint is quite thin. Or dilute various colors of India ink or prepare watercolors. Apply a wash of your chosen paint medium upon surface C (the tagboard). The deposited wax lines on surface C will resist the contrasting color(s) of diluted water crayon, India ink, or watercolor. Be certain that your tempera is thin enough. The thin wax lines will not resist if the paint is too thick. It might be wise to practice on scrap paper.

This approach has its limitations in that the design must be linear in nature. It is not easy to transfer solid areas of crayon by means of this process; a *direct* use of crayon on paper would be needed. Don't be afraid to draw parallel lines to suggest shading in a representational drawing.

You might wish to substitute wax paper for newsprint; since it is already coated with wax, it is not necessary to cover surface B solidly with crayon.

Illus. 239. Laundry blueing in liquid form was used as the painting medium. Observe that blueing is resisted by the wax lines most effectively.

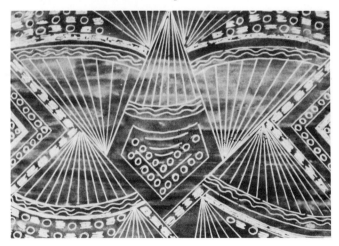

CHAPTER TEN

Exploring with Crayon Etching Technique

Illus. 240. This crayon etching reveals what beauty of line, color and pattern can be achieved with the sgraffito technique. The artist, a high school student, used a tracing paper outline to help him determine where the unetched black borders should be left between each colored shape.

Crayon etching is an adaptation of the sgraffito process, known since Renaissance times (perhaps before), whereby a surface is scratched or scraped revealing another colored surface below. While you make your crayon etchings, you will enjoy seeing how each new scratch of the sharp etching tool reveals a line or pattern of bright, warm color. The dark top surface seems to cry out for removal so that the hidden beauty of color beneath may receive an unveiling. It is the strong contrast—light, warm color beneath an inky blackness—that makes each line so very meaningful, so direct, so exciting to behold. Each effort produces results that are immediate, expressive and explicit.

Preparing the Surface

Creating the base of a crayon etching is simple. There are four surface covers: India ink, crayon, tempera and Magic Markers. Whatever cover you use, you must first color the entire surface of your background sheet with a layer of crayon, using one or many light, warm colors, juxtaposed. After your cover wash is painted over the crayoned surface and allowed to dry, use a sharp tool, such as a lead pencil point, to etch a design into the dark surface, being careful to reveal but not scratch the crayon color below.

If India ink is your covering medium, occasionally it will be resisted by the crayon so that you have to repaint a certain area repeatedly before it is properly covered. To speed up the process, pat a blackboard eraser containing chalk dust lightly upon the crayoned surface just prior to adding the India ink. India ink adheres more readily to a non-slick surface.

You might wish to experiment with India ink colors other than black, possibly even white, and reverse the usual color scheme of light showing through dark. Use dark colors of crayon on dark paper covered with a light-colored wash of India ink.

Since India ink is a permanent medium, it is difficult to remove from clothing and also a bit expensive. For these reasons, you might substitute black crayon, for example, which will produce a fine dark surface and is easy to rub over the lighter crayon colors.

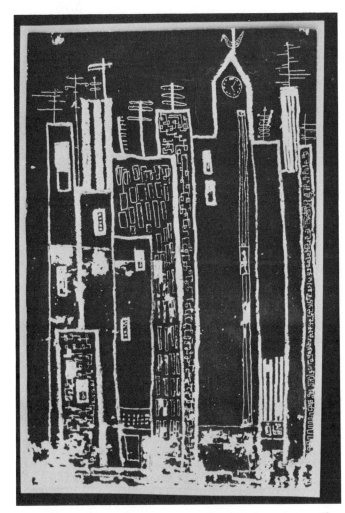

Illus. 241. There are a number of ways to prepare the surface of paper for the etching technique. Black tempera over crayon was used to create "The Skyscrapers." When tempera is used, the etched lines come out ragged.

Illus. 242. Nancy, a college student, decides to correlate all her etched lines with the color areas below her covering. The crayon design is carefully made on tagboard with wax crayons. Oil pastels could also have been used.

Illus. 243. Nancy places tracing paper over the finished crayon design and lightly traces and labels all color shapes because otherwise she will never be able to remember what is beneath the black India ink which she has chosen to use for her covering layer.

Illus. 244. She pats chalk dust with a blackboard eraser onto the glossy crayon surface so that the India ink will adhere more readily.

Illus. 245. The India ink adheres beautifully because of the dull chalk dust application underneath.

Illus. 246. Etching away.

A wash of dark tempera paint may also serve as a substitute for India ink. The crayoned surface will, of course, resist the tempera paint, as we know from Chapter 9. To prevent this, powdered tempera of the same color as the liquid wash should first be brushed onto the crayoned surface. Or, use chalk dust once again.

Another remedy for the problem of adherence is soap. First rub your brush across a wet cake of soap before painting with the liquid tempera. The wash will now spread evenly and effectively.

Liquid or powdered detergent might be added to the liquid tempera so as to achieve the same results. A raw potato might come to the rescue. Rub your brush across a sliced potato before painting with it on the crayoned surface.

Using tempera over crayon will cause your etched lines to come out less sharply and distinctly than with India ink. Evidence is found in Illus. 241, although here the somewhat ragged line enhances the etching.

All liquid washes (India ink or tempera) will cause the paper to buckle slightly. This, in turn, causes the wash to run down hill into the recessed areas of the paper. Remove this excess collection of liquid with your brush as the puddles will crack when dry. It is most difficult if not impossible to etch through an extra thick layer of dry India ink.

Try using a Magic Marker when covering your waxed

Illus. 247. The finished design. Before finishing it, Nancy lays the tracing paper periodically over the design as she etches (see Illus. 243) to remind her which shapes are to remain unetched. A second application of India ink can be used to cover any etching mistakes.

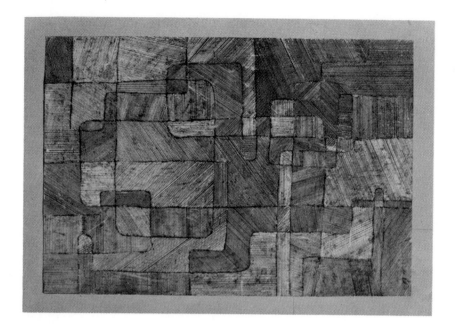

Illus. 248. A very narrow border is left between each shape here. The placements are determined by the design previously outlined on tracing paper. Note that the etching lines in each rectangle are at a different angle.

crayon surface. Black will prove most popular, but the artist will enjoy experimenting with other colors. You will discover that certain light colors do not cover well, whereas others are truly opaque.

Planned Color-Placement

Most beginners will prefer to create an unplanned color design. That is, they will etch lines at random, not taking into account which light color shapes lie beneath the dark outer layer. It is possible, however, to directly correlate all etched lines and patterns with certain designated colors, should an experienced student desire to do this. Illus. 242 through 247 show how planned color-placement may be carried out.

The planned approach was also used in Illus. 248. All of the rectangular shapes were traced on paper prior to the India ink application. Observe the different directions which the etched lines take. Some are diagonal, while others run in a parallel, vertical or horizontal direction. And each rectangular shape is divided by a narrow black border which was left during the etching procedure.

Correcting Errors

If you feel that you have made an error in etching, it can easily be rectified. India ink, crayon, tempera or the Magic Marker may be applied a second time to certain areas so as to cover the unwanted etched lines, making possible a second attempt in drawing.

Background Paper and Etching Tools

Manila paper works well as a background for crayon etching, but tagboard has the advantage of being smoother and thicker. Also sharp etching tools will not tear the surface of tagboard quite as easily.

Use an assortment of scratching and scraping tools to get variety in your lines and patterns. Use different tools in a single etching so as to achieve interesting, varied effects. Try working with a section of a hair comb or a silver fork for rhythmic, evenly-spaced, flowing lines. Try using the blunt end of a needle, the sharp edge of a narrow-headed screwdriver, a bobby pin, hairpin, a nut pick, the point of a nail, the point of a nail file, or a linoleum-block tool for making delicate lines. Search the

Illus. 249. Pamela, a fifth-grade student, has decided to use the simpler, unplanned color-placement approach in executing her etching. She juxtaposes shapes in yellow and pink for her underlayer of crayon.

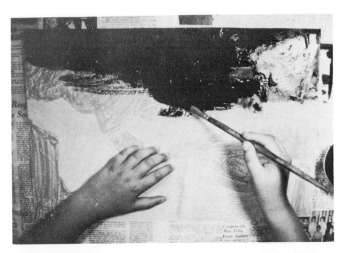

Illus. 250. She applies a wash of black India ink over the whole crayoned surface.

kitchen and garage for tools. A paring knife or a single-edged razor blade is especially effective in removing large areas of the dark surface.

Preserving Your Crayon Etchings

Finished crayon-etched designs are quite vulnerable to damage. An accidental scratch in the wrong place can easily mar the finished design. To preserve the etching, cover the completed work with a coat of white shellac or light varnish.

Unplanned Color-Placement

The color results in the unplanned color-placement approach are nearly always pleasing when light crayon colors are covered by a dark wash. Colors seldom clash with one another because the dominant black surface subdues the multi-colored surface below.

All the illustrations on this page show how a fifth-grade student from the Wyoming (Michigan) Parkview

Illus. 251. When Pamela scratches into the India ink surface with the sharp point of her pencil, she is etching a design. The colors pop up at random as no attempt has been made to correlate etched lines or shapes with the color shapes below.

School carries out her etching. Pamela leaves the etched patterns surrounded by solid black borders. The pinks

Illus. 252. Wide, bold lines make this flower stand out against the patterned background.

Illus. 253. Two beautiful fish with fancy scales swim about the ocean floor, between seaweed and reddish ocean plants in this fantasia of an unplanned crayon etching.

and yellows pop up wherever the etched lines allow them to.

As for subject matter for etching, Mother Nature suggests many ideas. Consider trees, flowers and plants, especially leaves and petals, their shapes, their vein patterns, their irregular edges. Consider the bent, curved stems which support blossoms and leaves and cause them to dance about in the breeze. And how interesting the blossom might become when it contains a long, protruding stamen and radiating, patterned petals.

A simple flower and stem are pictured in Illus. 252. The variety of pattern causes this simple design to come to life. Observe that the lines which define the stem and petals are wider and bolder than the many lines of the surrounding patterns.

An underwater scene, complete with patterned fish, detailed seaweed and other plant life, sponges, shells, castles, mermaids and other imaginary creatures might be fun to create by means of crayon etching. In Illus. 253, observe the many interesting patterns which suggest the fishes' scale formations. The delicate, finely etched strokes visible in the bottom plants provide a pleasing contrast to the bolder lines which outline and decorate the two fish.

Flying insects are fascinating to depict in a crayon etching. Consider their colorful, patterned wings and long, furry, patterned bodies, protruding antennae, bulging eyes and many crawling legs and feet. Consider the symmetry of an insect's design. Create an imaginary insect design, such as the delicate long-winged butterflies stylistically portrayed in Illus. 254.

Illus. 254. The flight of butterflies inspired the artist to make this abstraction. Observe the wing shapes pictured throughout the design. Delicate leaf and flower designs help to fill the lower negative spaces, uniting beautifully with the insect forms.

Birds, either real or imaginary, provide another fascinating subject for crayon etching. Illus. 256 is an imaginary bird created by an adult student who had a peacock in mind when creating her work. But she took

Illus. 256. The artist has taken artistic liberties with the peacock here. Imaginary birds provide interesting subjects for depiction in fine line etchings.

Illus. 255. A third-grade Kalamazoo student using the unplanned color approach created this Spring scene of the first robin pulling a long juicy worm from a colorful earth. The robin got a multi-color pattern etched upon his back, feathers and tail, while multi-color clouds float above.

Illus. 258. A country church stands amid the glories of nature.

Illus. 257. Artistic liberties were taken with this tree form. Electrifying branches flow from a massive trunk. The negative areas complement the active lines beautifully.

many liberties, as an artistic design was of more importance to her than a biologically correct representation. Observe the beautiful line patterns which adorn the bird's body, tail feathers and head. And observe that there is a pleasing relationship between the positive shape of the bird and the negative shapes which surround it. The dark unetched areas provide the eye with resting points so that the design does not become too busy; they serve to accentuate the bird.

Illus. 257 is not a real-looking tree, but it is certainly beautifully conceived. Electrifying roots and branches flame from the massive trunk, and an oversized knothole adorns the trunk. The long, narrow sheet of paper provides the perfect shape for depicting a subject such as this. Paper, cut into unusual shapes, will often suggest new and exciting ideas to the practicing artist.

"The Church in the Wildwood" (Illus. 258) was suggested by the familiar hymn of the same title and gave the artist an opportunity to portray a scene from nature.

Illus. 259 (left). One single color—white—was placed beneath the India ink covering here. It is not necessary to have a multi-color underlayer. This is like a commercial scratchboard.

Illus. 261 (above) and Illus. 262 (below). Imaginary views from a helicopter. Uniquely shaped fields are imagined as seen from above, by junior high school students.

Illus. 260 (left). This feathery design expresses a radial balance—that is, all lines radiate from the central focal point. They might suggest the twirling motions of a lawn sprinkler.

Illus. 263. Functional vases and other containers are made by placing a crayon-etched design around tin cans and cardboard cartons. (Left to right) A coffee can, an oatmeal carton, and a gallon-sized milk carton are covered with excitingly etched crayon designs.

Illus. 264 (far left) and 265 (below). These flat designs were created by fifth-grade students for covering quart-sized milk cartons. They were studying American Indians and were impressed by the geometric designs found on Indian blankets, jewelry and pottery.

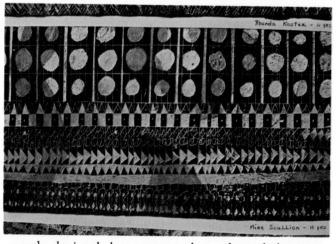

Crayon-Etched "Aerial Views"

A class of junior high students created imaginary designs in Illus. 261 and 262 suggested by an imaginary ride in a helicopter. Neat rectangular fields were most frequently depicted, but some students showed that some fields could suggest the curving, parallel lines of freshly cultivated earth. Many plowing formations and uniquely shaped fields came into existence as imaginations became activated.

Crayon-Etched Containers

Crayon etchings can decorate such useful articles as a vase, wastebasket, scrap box, yarn box or hair curler box. Select an appropriately sized and shaped cardboard carton, such as a circular oatmeal box, ice cream carton or gallon or half-gallon empty milk carton. Cut a large

Illus. 266 and 267. Your crayon-etched design on tagboard need not always be placed around a container. The stiff material will stand by itself when creased with two vertical folds into such shapes as the triangle (far left) or rolled into a cylinder. Join the ends of the tagboard with heavy wire staples or brass paper fasteners to complete these "stabiles."

Illus. 268. This crayon-etched collage was made by cutting interesting shapes from single-color crayon etchings and pasting them onto a background of contrasting color.

sheet of tagboard to size so that it will completely surround the carton. The design may be etched upon the tagboard while it is around the carton or in a removed, flat position.

The flat repeat designs created by fifth-grade students in Illus. 264 and 265 were inspired by prints, filmstrips and films displaying American Indian crafts. The Indian designs were geometric and repeated frequently. With all of the illustrative aids put away, the students proceeded to make their own creations. Some students used a ruler to achieve straight lines. The finished, flat designs were stapled around the empty milk cartons and a coat of clear shellac was added to preserve the etched designs.

Crayon-Etched "Stabiles"

If your tagboard creations are strong enough to stand by themselves, you can make "stabiles" as shown in Illus. 266 and 267.

Crayon-Etched Collages

An interesting collage may be made from your etched designs and patterns. In Illus. 268, for example, various designs were etched on separate sheets of tagboard—one undercolor per sheet—then cut into interesting shapes and glued to a background of black construction paper. The yellow border effectively repeats the yellow colors within the design.

Crayon-Etched Name Designs

Names provide exciting motifs for execution by crayon etching. Decorate the various letters with intricate line designs, and surround the name with bold patterns.

Illus. 269. Donnette used her name as her dominant motif, and embellished it with a variety of intricate line designs. She surrounded these delicately etched patterns with bold waves and stripes.

Illus. 270 and 271. The etching technique was used here to simulate the stained glass windows. Illus. 270 (left): Crayoned color areas are placed so that the natural white paper provides a plain border between each shape. Illus. 271 (right): Black India ink has been applied. All shapes are etched so that the crayon color comes through. The separating borders become black from the ink since no crayon was placed in these areas.

Simulated Stained Glass Window Etchings

In using tagboard with the crayon etching technique to execute a simulated stained glass window, the transparent quality of the glass must be sacrificed, but the design qualities of the window may be effectively simulated.

The stained glass window rose in popularity during the 12th century when the Gothic cathedral was at its height. Large architectural openings were filled with brilliant, colored, luminous, transparent glass designs. The earliest windows made use of few colors—blue, yellow, and red. Later, more colors were invented and used, and this started the decline of stained glass windows. A window design is most pleasing when a few colors are frequently repeated within the composition. A small range of color causes the design to achieve a unity of its parts, while the repetition allows the artist to balance his colors.

The earliest window designs were rather crude in concept. The French artist of the 12th century planned his cathedral window by drawing thin black lines to indicate the iron and lead tracings which held the transparent shapes of glass in place, against wind and storms. The lead and iron tracings usually cut through the faces, hands and legs of figures in a most disconcerting way. Through experience, the artist learned to manipulate his framework so that the glass shapes were not sacrificed.

Stained glass has its limitations. It does not allow the artist to achieve the illusion of depth. Stained windows echo the Cubistic style of early 20th century painting in that shapes cling to a flat 2-dimensional surface. Also stained glass does not allow the artist to create highly representational designs. Photographic likenesses of

Illus. 273. After this Madonna was etched on thin white paper, it was coated on the back with linseed oil to make a more transparent etching for a stained glass window.

Illus. 274 and 275 demonstrate the Christmas passage from the Bible: "And there were shepherds in the same country abiding in the field, and keeping watch by night over their flock. And an angel of the Lord stood by them, and the glory of the Lord shone round about them; and they were sore afraid."

people, for example, cannot be achieved. Toward the end of the Gothic movement, a few artists attempted to represent realistic figures in 3 dimensions but such attempts also led to the decline of the stained glass window technique. You must be aware of the limitations of any technique and material if your final design is to be aesthetic.

Two approaches may be used in executing a simulated stained glass design. In Illus. 270, the artist applied blue, green and yellow crayons to his tagboard, carefully retaining a border of uncolored paper between each colored shape. When the over-coat of black India ink was dry, he used a sharp pencil point to etch lines across the inked surface, distinctly revealing the solid shapes of colored crayon (Illus. 271). The now-black borders vividly define each color shape.

Using the second approach, in Illus. 272 the artist colored black borders between each light colored area with a black crayon. India ink was applied over all and partly etched away when dry. The black crayoned borders remain quite vivid in spite of the etching process. He re-crayoned in black where too much black was etched away by accident.

Colorful stained glass windows often remind us of the Christmas season. And since the etchings in Illus. 273 through 279 were created during the Christmas season, it is not surprising to find that Christmas motifs adorn each design. In Illus. 273, the Madonna is surrounded by blue, aqua and purple shades of color. This design was made upon thin white paper and painted (upon the rear side) with a coat of linseed oil, which caused the paper to become more transparent. When placed against

The traditional poinsettia provides Illus. 277 with its decorative motif. The red blossoms are surrounded by yellow, blue and green. An interesting textural pattern is established by nature of the etching procedure.

White Christmas candles, backed by a mosaic-like pattern of green, red, blue and yellow shapes are visible in Illus. 279. In Illus. 278, the Madonna views the Christ child wrapped in swaddling clothes, lying in a manger.

Illus. 277. The traditional poinsettia provides the dominant motif in this window design.

Illus. 276. A church and surrounding objects reveal many interesting, variegated shapes, both in size and pattern.

a windowpane, the colors of the etched lines became quite intense in color.

A church is pictured in Illus. 276. Observe the many sectional patterns which decorate the church, grass, sky and tree. The shapes display a fine variance in size as they are inspected from area to area.

The traditional poinsettia again provides the dominant motif in Illus. 280. Many diverse colored blossoms are tightly woven between interesting geometric shapes of color.

Illus. 279. Nine Christmas candles are backed by a mosaic-like pattern.

Illus. 278. An interpretation of the Madonna fondling her newborn child.

Illus. 280. Modern-looking poinsettia blossoms are positioned amidst a tightly woven pattern of geometrically etched shapes.

Illus. 281 (below). Marcia's bottom sheet has been covered smoothly with a layer of yellow chalk and then a layer of dark crayon. When Marcia places a clean sheet of paper over this and presses hard with her pencil in sketching a line design, she discovers that the underside of the top sheet is picking up a transfer and, moreover, is leaving a neat design in reverse colors on the under sheet!

Crayon-on-Chalk Transfer Etchings

A beautiful negative-positive etching may be executed with the use of chalk and crayon, and you can create two designs in one operation.

To begin, get two sheets of manila or white drawing paper identical in size. Cover one of the sheets with a heavy coat of yellow chalk. Next, heavily apply a layer of dark crayon so that the chalk is completely covered. Next, lay your clean sheet over the crayoned sheet. Using a sharp pencil, draw a design upon the uncolored sheet. Press hard and work on a hard-surfaced desk or table so that the transfer etching will be distinct. Create line patterns only, but don't be afraid to shade your objects with parallel line patterns or cross-hatch designs. When you remove the top sheet, you will discover that the pencil drawing has caused the crayon wax to leave the chalk backing, and that delicate crayon lines have been lifted and transferred to the underside of your top sheet (see Illus. 281). Mount both parts of your positive-negative design side by side since they have the same colors (but in reverse). (See also Illus. 284 and 285.)

140

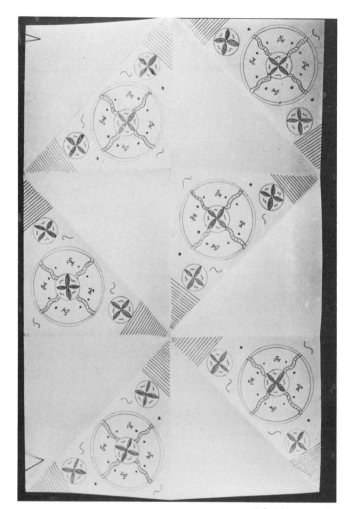

Illus. 282 and 283. An ingenious system of folding and coloring was followed, using only one sheet of paper, to create a transfer etched design. (See text.)

Illus. 282 and 283 demonstrate how a complicated folding technique can be used to create a transfer etching upon a single sheet of paper, not upon separate sheets of paper. Vertical, horizontal and diagonal creases were first folded into the paper. Then chalk covered by crayon was applied to alternate triangles (Illus. 282, left). Using the central, vertical fold as his dividing line, the artist

made sure that his crayoned triangles on the left would face an uncrayoned shape on the right, when the paper was again folded in half, along the central vertical crease. A line design was pressed upon the reverse side of the vertically-folded sheet now but applied only over those triangles which were covered with chalk and crayon. As you can see in Illus. 283, the two green crayoned triangles

Illus. 284 (left). Four squares were colored on a chalked sheet with different color crayons. When a line design was drawn on the opposite side of an overlaid sheet of paper, a transfer design (Illus. 285, right) was obtained. (Also see Illus. 281.)

Illus. 286. A black wash was painted over the entire crayoned surface of this flower arrangement leaving a bubbly design upon the wax surface.

Illus. 287. First a line was scraped through a solid layer of wax crayon to create this design by a student from Holland, Michigan. Then a wash of black tempera filled the etched line with contrasting color.

on the left deposited a green line pattern upon triangles to the right. The single green triangle on the right hand side deposited a green line design on the corresponding shape to the left. The solid orange shapes have likewise left their imprint upon the opposite side. This technique of working is too complicated for children of elementary grades.

142

Painted Line Etchings

To paint a line etching, start by covering a smooth sheet of paper completely with a layer of wax crayon or oil pastel. One color or a combination of colors may be used. With a sharp tool, such as the point of a nail file,

Illus. 288. In this floral design, black was painted over an etched line design, and care was taken not to paint the unlined crayoned areas.

Illus. 289. Two crayon colors, orange and yellow, were used to create "City Skyline."

scratch a line design through the crayon layer. Press the tool hard enough to remove the crayon film, but not so hard as to tear the paper. Next, paint a wash of black (or other dark color) tempera over the scratched design. The tempera will adhere only to those areas where lines have been scratched through, and will leave a deposit of small bubbles where the wax remains.

While it is usual to paint the black tempera over the entire crayoned area, the tempera in Illus. 288 was

Illus. 290. "Autumn Leaves" was colored in solid tones of green, orange and yellows. A subtle line was etched among the shapes to define some of the leaf shapes and to convey the leaves' vein patterns. Note the pattern of black bubbles created during the wash application.

Illus. 292. By pressing extra hard upon white drawing paper, the artist created an etching which came out quite distinctly after applying crayon. He colored certain shapes, as designated by the etched line design.

Illus. 291. Katherine has used a nut pick to press an embossed line design upon a sheet of paper, with other sheets placed below to serve as a soft padding. Now she is rubbing a dark crayon across the paper's surface to bring out the embossed lines.

painted over the etched lines only, keeping the (golden) background as clean as possible.

In "City Skyline" (Illus. 289) two colors of crayon were used. The deep orange tones are placed around the etched lines of the skyscrapers, spotlights and vertical line patterns. A black water crayon was dissolved and used to darken the lines.

Embossed Line Etchings

Place your sheet of paper upon a cushion of papers, such as a thin pad of newspaper or a few sheets of manila paper. For this, you are interested in imprinting an uncolored, embossed line upon your paper, not a pencil line or a crayon line. A nut pick will do nicely as a tool, but any pointed instrument that is sharp enough to press a deep line without leaving a dark line or tearing the paper will do. After completing the embossed line design, rub a dark crayon over the entire surface of the design, *across* your embossed lines and not *with* the lines. Do not press heavily, or the embossed lines will get filled with color. When finished, you will observe that the natural color of the paper is retained where the embossed lines have been placed. All other areas will be colored with crayon.

Illus. 293. Green construction paper and white crayon were used to create this embossed line etching. White crayon was rubbed heavily along the side of some of the embossed lines to emphasize them.

Illus. 294. All negative shapes were cut away and the positive forms glued to a contrasting sheet of black construction paper, in this combination combining the collage-embossed line etching. Note that this is practically the same basic tulip drawing as Illus. 293.

If the strokes of the crayon are too weak to show up the embossed lines distinctly, re-crayon some of the shapes. You will then have a background consisting of two shades of color—a light dark and a darker dark.

Combining Collage and Embossing

Being pleased with the tulip design in Illus. 293, the artist decided to make a second similar design which combined the embossed etching technique with the collage technique. The embossed line was again pressed onto green construction paper and white crayon was rubbed over the lines. But in Illus. 294 all negative areas of the design were cut away so that the positive shapes might be glued to a contrasting sheet of black construction paper. The etched lines are very much in evidence when viewing the tulip blossoms.

Melted Crayon Etchings

Illus. 295 demonstrates what sharp, distinct lines may be achieved when etching with melted wax crayon. Select two contrasting colors of wax crayon and melt each color separately, using any one of the melting procedures

Illus. 295. Two contrasting colored layers of melted wax crayon were painted on tagboard to create this etching. A pencil point was used to etch the design, revealing the darker color below.

Illus. 296. Both the crayon resist and the crayon etching techniques were used to execute this design. The etching technique was used to create the colorful border; the resist technique was responsible for the central tulip design.

suggested in Chapter 8. Using a stiff bristle brush, paint one color of melted crayon over tagboard, manila paper, white drawing paper or cardboard, completely covering its surface. When the first layer of wax has hardened, paint on the second color. Next, using a sharp instrument, etch a line design through the top layer so the contrasting color below becomes visible.

Combining Crayon Resist and Etching

In a crayon etching, you use black India ink and bright crayon colors. And when creating a crayon resist drawing, the desired result is bright color against a dark background. So it would only seem logical that both techniques might be combined within a single composition. And indeed they can, as shown in Illus. 296 and 297.

The central rectangular shape in Illus. 296, a tulip design, including decorative leaves and a dotted design surrounding the flower, has been executed by means of the crayon resist technique. Black tempera was painted over the crayon line design. The colorful border which surrounds the inner rectangle was executed by means of the crayon etching technique. A solid border of two colors—red and blue—was crayoned on the paper and covered with India ink. Then a ruler and sharp etching tool were used to etch the crossed-line design, revealing the red and blue crayon colors beneath the black ink. The two crayon techniques were beautifully combined to create a single composition.

The palm tree design has been simply divided into positive and negative areas with one technique serving the positive shapes and the other technique decorating the negative areas. The tree trunk and all palm leaves were executed by means of the etching technique. All of the spaces which fall in between are decorated with the crayon relief technique.

Throughout this book we have made an attempt to illustrate the fact that the crayon is truly a versatile tool. In each chapter we have tried to substantiate this belief.

Illus. 297. All positive palm leaf shapes were etched in this example. All negative areas were decorated with the resist technique.

As you make further explorations with the crayon, you will see how true this fact is. Experience teaches that new and exciting ideas continually come into existence as you involve yourself with this remarkable art tool. There is no end to the possibilities presented by this medium. The crayon is truly a versatile tool!

Illus. 298. A second-grader in the Kalamazoo public schools gives his conception of a tree gained from a "looking walk." It is autumn, leaves are falling, and the tree's skeleton is very much in evidence. Bees sing lazily in the heat of a late September sun. A large white knot hole is recalled. Observe the interesting pattern the young artist has established in the trunk and branches. Crayons have served the artist well.

CHAPTER ELEVEN

What Shall We Draw?

"What shall we draw?" is an important classroom question which needs to be answered in a meaningful way. Children cannot create in a vacuum. They must be stimulated to think of their experiences, thoughts and feelings and to express these experiences in art.

The class excursion is one of the most appropriate avenues to provide common experiences for all pupils. You might wish to refer to it as a "looking walk." The crayon drawing stimulated by the excursion can be a window into the mind of each student. He will draw those objects which impressed him most during the outing, eliminating the non-essentials. Trips to the museum, pet shop, aquarium, park, farm, fruit market, flower nursery, firehouse and dairy also would provide much food for creative thought.

Invite children to examine things—to feel the trunk of a tree, for example, to throw their arms around it. Allow children to experience the magnitude of a large tree, the frailty of a small tree.

Perhaps the looking walk will draw students' attention to the details of homes and buildings. You might stop and take a close look at one. Observe the interesting shingle patterns which adorn the roof, the flower garden, details of windows and front door.

After children return from their summer vacations is the time to discuss the many pleasant experiences they had, in preparation for crayon activity. The teacher does not have time to hear all of his students describe their summer, but as a few answer the questions, all the class will be stimulated to consider their own chosen activity for creative art.

Illus. 299. A sixth-grade student has masterfully combined crayon with watercolor during an on-the-spot sketching excursion. The tree trunks, branches, and outline and detail of the home have been rendered in crayon. A resisting watercolor wash was added to color the windows, lawn and foliage.

Illus. 300. Almost every classroom has a collector of insects. Encourage students to bring their insect collections to class, and observe the insects' shapes, colors, symmetry. This crayon resist drawing by a fourth-grade student was inspired by the study of insects and plants.

Illus. 301. Inspired by a magnifying-glass view of nature, this was created by a fifth-grade student from the Kalamazoo public schools to represent plant cells.

Illus. 302. An exciting moment in a football game, re-called by a sixth-grade student. Numerous spectators in even rows view a tackle. Note the perspective (or lack of it) in the stairway.

Illus. 303. An imaginary bird from another planet, seen from the window of a space capsule. Sixth-grade students from the Granville (Mich.) Public Schools imagined they were astronauts taking an imaginary ride through space. Observe the many interesting patterns which adorn the strange bird's body. The side of a peeled crayon was used to add background tones and clouds.

Reading aloud a well chosen story can provide another avenue to stimulate children to express ideas with crayon. It allows each child to identify with the characters in the story. Be sure the incidents seem credible.

Children's phonograph records provide an excellent source for stimulating children to draw with crayon because the background sounds and music produce a mood.

The study of science affords many opportunities to correlate drawing activities with new experiences. Children have a natural interest in animals, insects and plants. Animal antics might suggest humorous expression in a crayon drawing. Both the microscope and the magnifying glass will prove indispensable in exploring science and art. Encourage older students to view, for example, the veins of a leaf, the wing of an insect, the skin of a snake and stained specimens through the microscope. The artist will see new lines, colors, textures, patterns and shapes. A whole new horizon is opened up. Students of the elementary grades will enjoy taking a looking walk with a magnifying glass in hand.

Sports events provide yet another source of inspiration for expression in art. Children perform in the gymnasium and playground, and their favorite games may be depicted in crayon drawings. Students are also spectators at exciting sports events.

Young children live in a comparatively small world, consisting of family, playmates, pets and teacher. Family activities hold special meaning for them and provide experiences to be expressed in art.

Children are not afraid to draw imaginary situations because they realize that objects cannot be drawn incorrectly. How can anyone criticize a drawing when it is not based on reality?

The older student might wish to base his imagined drawing on some exciting event. Perhaps the student imagines herself at her own wedding. A young child might wish to portray himself as an adult. Perhaps he is a

Illus. 304. A third-grade student imagines himself to be a famous circus clown, entertaining throngs of admiring people. There he is, in the spotlight, dressed in long funny brown shoes and tall hat. How the people laugh as they watch him perform!

Illus. 305. Hallowe'en is a time to think of ghosts and goblins. In this crayon drawing by a fifth-grade student from the Kalamazoo (Mich.) Public Schools, entitled "Tree Ghosts," on Hallowe'en night the trees take on the appearance of ghosts.

famous movie star, a rock and roll singer, a TV comedian, or a circus performer.

Holidays and festive events provide opportunities to express ideas with crayon. Valentine's Day, for example, would provide the perfect opportunity for children to create colorful valentines with crayon and paper. A folded sheet of paper would permit the student to include a poem within the card. The card's cover might consist of a single valentine or a design composed of various-sized valentines. The crayon relief technique might be used to imprint a lacy design around the valentine's edges.

The Christmas season provides another perfect opportunity to draw scenes which reflect the activities associated with this joyous season. Drawings might re-veal the family picking out a Christmas tree, decorating the tree, hanging the Christmas stockings, exchanging gifts, attending the Christmas church service, eating Christmas dinner. Crayon drawings might portray scenes from well-known Christmas carols.

Hallowe'en is the time to draw fierce-looking masks on paper or on paper bags which can be worn upon the head, the time to draw ghosts, goblins, witches, cats and graveyards.

Thanksgiving is a time to reflect upon the many spiritual and material blessings we have. At Easter time, people wear new clothes. Stimulate children to draw portraits of themselves or their mother, father, brother or sister all dressed up.

CHAPTER TWELVE

How to Mount Your Crayon Drawings

A crayon drawing is not ready to exhibit until it has been matted or framed. A border adds the finishing touch.

In choosing a frame, there are two considerations. First, the frame must relate well to the composition of your drawing. Second, it should relate well with its surroundings—the decor of the room in which the drawing is to be exhibited. Actually, both the mounted drawing and the frame must relate well with their environment, with the frame providing a transition between the artistic composition and the wall.

When choosing a colored mat or frame, think of the effect the mat will have upon the crayon design. Paper mats with a flat, non-glare surface and neutral color, such as black, white and grey, usually harmonize well with any colored design. They place emphasis on the design's colors and in no way distract from them. White, black and grey frames afford easy transition to the surrounding wall and room objects. Neutral-colored frames will cause a design weak in color to appear stronger. A frame that is intense in color would draw too much attention, would decrease the strength of a weak-colored design and over-power it.

If your crayon drawing is strongly colored and you want to mat it with a colored frame, you might consider repeating the colors of your composition in the mat you choose. The border can repeat the color most frequently used within the composition—or the color which is used

Illus. 306. This crayon etching was framed in oak. Note the paper border which is wider at top and bottom than on the sides. Two shades of blue echo small areas of similar color within the design.

the least. Paper mats which echo both the dominant and restricted colors of the design should be placed next to the art work to see which relates best in conjunction with the room. It is quite possible that you might wish to repeat both the dominant and restricted colors of your design in your chosen mat. A number of color plates in this book illustrate the use of double-colored mats.

You might wish to have the bottom border of your mat deeper than the top and certainly greater than the side borders. A slight increase in the bottom margin serves to offset the visual weight balance. If the bottom is equal in depth to the top, it tends to appear narrower than the top when displayed on the wall. However, with a non-representational design, a mat with four even-width sides would allow you to position it in any manner you desire—horizontally, vertically or even upside-down, provided it looks right that way.

Paper Mounts and Matboards

Most of the illustrations in this book were simply pasted over one, two or more sheets of construction paper which serve as the mat. White liquid glue (Elmer's glue) provides an effective, lasting adhesive.

A 14-ply matboard, available in white, black, grey, warm and cool colors, might be used to create an inexpensive and professional-appearing frame. Using a sharp cutting instrument, cut your matboard to the required height and width. Next, cut a window through the middle at least ¼ inch smaller (on all four sides) than your design.

The width of all four sides of your mat (with the bottom slightly greater) should correlate well with the size of your design. A frame that is too great in size distracts from your art work. A skimpy, narrow frame tends to demean your design.

Place your crayon design against the back side of your cut matboard so that the design shows through the window. Using gummed or cellophane tape, secure your design to the back side of the board. Run tape along all sides, but end it a few inches from each of the four corners to prevent warpage.

You might wish to cover your matboard. Velvet, burlap, metallic cloth, paper with a patterned crayon relief or resist design, or other material might be glued over the front. Cut your material large enough to be able to bend it over the edges of your cardboard mat. Diluted white liquid glue will provide the perfect adhesive.

The finished matboard, with design attached, might be glued down on a piece of cardboard to provide extra stability. Cut the cardboard just slightly smaller than the outer dimensions of your matboard. Do not place glue on the back of your design as this may cause the paper to wrinkle, but place a narrow stripe of glue about one inch from the outer edges of the rear side of the matboard.

Wood and Metal Frames

You might wish to place your matted design within a thin wooden or metal frame. A backing of cardboard would not be needed if a wooden or metal frame is used, as the frame will supply the needed stability. Also, most of the purchased frames contain a cardboard backing of their own which you might loosely attach to the back side.

Your crayon designs may simply be mounted over a number of other materials, all of which should be cut slightly larger than your design. For instance, your drawing might be pasted over a thin sheet of plywood. Using oil crayons and turpentine, stain the wood so that its grain is effectively emphasized. The design might also be placed over a sheet of wallboard. Using enamels or acrylics, paint the board the color of your choice. Cork in sheet form is available from many arts and crafts suppliers and would provide an interesting frame for certain designs, or cork can be used with other materials to provide a double frame. Tagboard might provide a simple frame in some instances. Its tan, neutral color blends with many colors and, being somewhat stiff, it could well provide the necessary support for your smaller designs.

Index

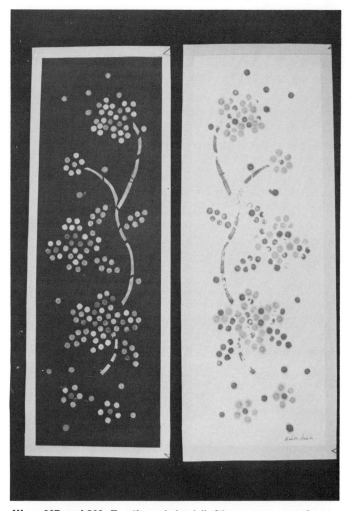

Illus. 307 and 308. For the original (left), a paper punch was used to create the small circular shapes out of crayoned sheets of paper. These were arranged in this Oriental design and newsprint was laid over the whole sheet. When a warm flatiron pressed the newsprint against the wax-crayon art it caused the wax to transfer from the original to the newsprint (right).

Illus. 309. Creating many open patterns on paper for future use.

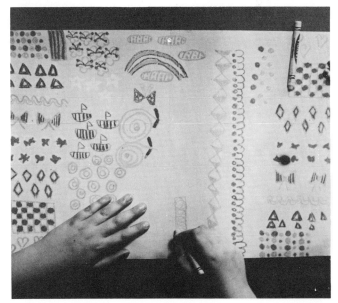

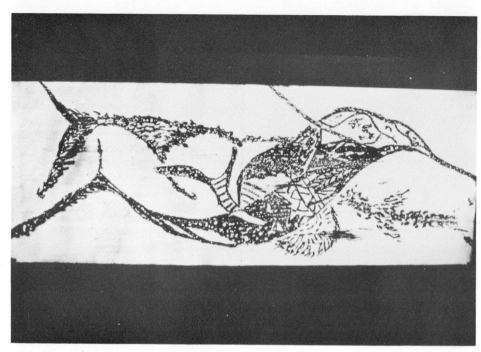

Illus. 310. Is it a bird or is it a fish? This non-representational design is on two sheets of dark blue construction paper joined end to end.

THE AUTHOR

For many years Chester Jay Alkema has taught art to children of the Seymour Christian School, Grand Rapids, Michigan, and the Wyoming Parkview School, Wyoming, Michigan. Since 1959 he has taught adult art education courses for Michigan State University in East Lansing, Grand Rapids, Benton Harbor and Niles, Michigan. In the spring of 1965, Prof. Alkema joined the art faculty of Grand Valley State College, Allendale, Michigan, and is now Assistant Professor of Fine Arts.

A graduate of Calvin College, Grand Rapids, Michigan, Prof. Alkema received a M.A. in Art and a M.A. in Fine Arts from Michigan State University. He has contributed many articles to educational publications. Almost all photographs in the book were taken by the author.